EVERY GARDEN TELLS
A STORY

To Linda
1948 was a good year for
you Prince Charles and myself
were born.

EVERY GARDEN TELLS
A STORY

G. Elliott

George Elliott

Book Guild Publishing

Sussex, England

First published in Great Britain in 2012 by
The Book Guild Ltd
Pavilion View
19 New Road
Brighton, BN1 1UF

Typesetting in Garamond by
Keyboard Services, Luton, Bedfordshire

Printed in Great Britain by
CPI Group (UK) Ltd, Croydon, CR0 4YY

A catalogue record for this book is available from
The British Library

ISBN 978 1 84624 787 3

To Woofy

Contents

Acknowledgements

I would like to thank the following people who, for many reasons, made the writing of this book possible.

My family, and Max.
Lady Scarsdale.
The Hon Richard Curzon.
The Hon James Curzon.
Ray, Rosie and Henry.
Jane Brewster Beard.
Susan Littleford.
Mrs M.P. Matthews.

1

Heart of England

Aswan, Egypt, 1988

Back on board the *Nile Princess*, it was time to relax.

The locals had gathered at the riverbank to peddle their wares, bartering and haggling as only Egyptians can, trying to sell us the usual stuff – papyrus, Egyptian cotton and some rare and ancient artefacts with a dubious provenance. My attention was drawn to an elderly gentleman with a hand cart. It was laden with the fruits of his labour, and judging by the few simple tools he had, he must have been a small-time farmer, or possibly a gardener like myself. Whoever he was, we had something in common; we earned our living off the land.

He was small, with smiling eyes that danced around in the fading light, searching our faces, eagerly looking for another sale. His toothless grin reminded me of someone I knew years ago. It was Cyril, an old workmate of mine, back in the days when I was just starting out. Under his guidance, I spent some of my early days not only learning the trade but also one or two hard lessons in manners and respect. Lessons I'd never forget.

With last minute bargains secured, I watched the little fellow trundle off into the night. I couldn't help but feel a little envious of his simple way of life; a life that seemed to be free from the cares of the modern world.

His was an ancient land where life has changed little over thousands of years. A land of heat and desert, its people clinging to an emerald thread of the life created by the waters of the world's mightiest river – the Nile.

Romantic as it was, I still wouldn't swap it for the stormy skies of England and my way of life, working in the heart of the country in a land of green fields, pleasant towns and villages, and of course beautiful gardens.

Just like the Egyptian, my life as a gardener has been one of work, hard physical work, but it's also been a labour of love, giving me great pleasure and rich satisfaction. Unlike my counterpart, scraping a living along the banks of the Nile, Kath and I were beginning to enjoy the fruits of our labour.

It wasn't always so. There had been hard times – times when our future was uncertain. An old friend once gave me some invaluable words of wisdom; 'Don't forget, life is like a mirror. It'll reflect the effort you put into it.' And so it has been. After much hard work and determination, life was now beginning to reward us.

Our dream of travelling to Egypt had finally come true and we enjoyed every minute of it, but now it was time to get ready for the farewell party and the journey home.

I had tried working indoors, and it was like being suffocated. The prospect of spending the next fifty years stuck at a factory workbench or in some stuffy office didn't bear thinking about. To me, it would have been a prison sentence. One thing was clear above all else: I had to be outdoors, in some way connected with nature and the countryside.

The garden became my workplace; not one garden, but thousands. The last forty-five years have given me a unique opportunity to work in the gardens of some of the finest houses around. Gardens of every description from magnificent stately homes to quaint country cottages in quiet villages, to the bustling inner city and the gardens of suburbia, the gardens of industry, construction, clubs, pubs and giant corporations.

Look at a map of the world, and you will see Britain at its centre. Set in the heart of England is Derbyshire – the centre of the modern world.

Covering more than a thousand square miles, it's a place of green hills and pleasant valleys, watered by picturesque rivers. A land of natural beauty.

There are countless little villages and old market towns, steeped in history and tradition. Many seem to be hidden from the world.

Wherever you live in Britain, you are never far from the sea. In fact the furthest point from the sea is in Derbyshire, at Church Flats Farm near the village of Coton-in-the-Elms, seventy miles from the edge of the Wash in Lincolnshire.

As anyone who knows Derbyshire will tell you, it has everything; a place where every season has its delights.

Stone Age man settled here, as did the Romans, who mined Derbyshire lead. Some can be found in the ancient cities of Rome and Pompeii. The Danes, Saxons and Normans also left their mark on this beautiful landscape.

Derbyshire has played its part in shaping the modern world. Beside the River Derwent are some of the world's oldest factories. Britain's first silk mill is to be found in Derby, while at Cromford near Matlock, one of the leading figures of the industrial revolution, Sir Richard Arkwright, perfected the world's first water-powered cotton mill.

The oil industry was born in Ridding in 1847, when James Oakes erected the world's first oil refinery. Britain's first public park, the Arboretum, was laid out in Derby in 1840 and in the north of the county, the Peak District became Britain's first National Park in 1951.

In the south, lying in the lowlands of the Trent Valley is Repton, for centuries a famous seat of learning and once the capital of the Mercian Kingdom. It was here in AD 653 that Christianity was first preached in the Midlands.

'Bonny Prince Charlie stayed here' or 'Bonny Prince Charlie hid here' are claims I've heard more than once over the years from people whose homes lie along the route he took when his invading army passed through the county in 1745. After reaching the medieval Swarkestone Bridge that spans the River Trent in the south of the county, he made his retreat north, back to Scotland and defeat at Culloden.

John Flamsteed, the first Astronomer Royal, was a native of Derbyshire as was the artist Joseph Wright. Although she was born in Italy, Florence Nightingale's much-loved childhood home was at Lea Hurst near Matlock.

My journey around the English garden has been a long one. Many gardens are steeped in history and tradition, their owners coming from all walks of life and backgrounds. This has given me the opportunity to meet interesting people and work alongside many colourful characters, leaving lasting memories of days gone by. A few however, like garden pests, are quite nasty and best forgotten.

Over the years, working relationships have been forged and some have lasted for decades. The early 1980s saw the beginning of our long association with Rolls Royce, the famous aero-engine manufacturer of Derby.

The busy industrial landscape is a dramatic contrast to the peace and quiet of the countryside and places like Kedleston Hall, the ancestral home of the Curzon family, where I first worked in the gardens in the 1960s and continued to do so for many years to follow.

The story of life in a great house is a story of upstairs and downstairs, of butlers, cooks and housemaids serving their masters above with little mention of the world outside, the world of the gardeners, estate workers and people of the land. They also have a tale to tell but their stories are often lost in the pages of history. These are people whose wealth is not measured in material gain but in the glorious surroundings in which they work. Their rewards are of a different kind; being at one with nature and at peace with the world, and they are priceless.

There are so many stories it would be impossible to tell them all, but it is to my time at Kedleston that these pages are dedicated – to one day in particular, many years ago.

Kedleston Hall Derbyshire, 1976

The door burst open and a portly figure appeared, the soft glow of the fire lighting up an anguished face. It was Woofy, and he was not a happy man. 'All for a crust!', he boomed. His broad Yorkshire tones seemed to ring in our ears and bounce off the walls of the old gardener's shed. Cold and bedraggled, he was soaked to the skin, with a piece of old sacking hung across his shoulders in a vain attempt to keep out the driving rain. He looked for all the world like a throwback from another age. Puffing and wheezing, he struggled to unlace his soggy boots whilst casting a suspicious eye on Fred and me, sitting cosy and warm by the fire, having long since abandoned any thoughts of work.

'What are you two doing in here?' he barked. 'Let me guess. Skiving, I suppose?' Fred muttered some sarcastic remark about fools in the rain, which drew a less than friendly glance. I locked eyes with him to warn him off, trying to calm the situation; the last thing we needed was to upset Woofy. Thankfully it worked, because if he were in a mood, we would all suffer.

Although Fred and Woofy were around the same age, their backgrounds and characters couldn't have been more different. Ken Woof had worked the land all his life, most of it in farming. He was a countryman; Yorkshire born and bred and proud of it. He was in his late fifties when he took up the post of gardener for Lord and Lady Scarsdale, having spent all his life working on a variety of farms and estates up and down the country, but mostly in Yorkshire.

Woofy claimed to have seen Rudolf Hess, Adolf Hitler's second in command, on one occasion as he walked with his guards around a large estate during the war.

He was no stranger to hard work, but the life of a farm manager was becoming too much for him with only one Sunday off each month. The job at Kedleston meant shorter hours, weekends off and the work was lighter.

Being a typical Yorkshire man, Ken was cricket mad. Ken and

his wife Eileen lived in one of the mews flats above the old stabling block and livery rooms, to the west of the hall. When looking for some new carpet, he was delighted to find a piece that was twenty-two yards long, the length of a cricket pitch.

The mews were formally used by the livery staff and consisted of several rooms leading off one long corridor. Anything that moved, such as a washing machine or spin dryer, had to be tied down. If not, it would start to rattle its way across the uneven floors, heading towards the other side of the room. Invited to tea once, Kath and I watched in great amusement as a tomato fell from my plate, made its way across the room and out of the door.

He and Fred never quite saw eye to eye, which isn't surprising as until their paths crossed at the hall, their worlds had been poles apart.

Fred was a city man through and through, a Jack the lad with a wicked sense of humour, but despite all Woofy's doubts and concerns as to his character, Fred was the loyal type and was certainly someone who could be relied upon.

The old sea dog had served with the Royal Navy during the Second World War and by all accounts nearly came to grief at the hands of the Mafia in Sicily after some misdemeanour with a mobster's daughter. Knowing Fred as I did, I believed every word of it. He was lucky; being banged up on board for some minor offence, he was saved from the clutches of a vengeful father until the ship finally left port. He still swears he left behind a little Freda or Freddy walking the streets of Palermo.

'We're worse off than the Martyrs!' cried Woofy.

'Life isn't all that bad,' I said. 'Compared to the Martyrs, we've never had it so good. They really did work for a crust!' I wished I'd kept my mouth shut.

'Well at least they had a holiday in Australia, and some sunshine. But I can see life isn't that bad for some, is it?' he snapped. 'Not for the likes of you two, sitting on your backsides doing nothing.'

It had been a miserable morning. That summer had been one

of the hottest on record, with little rain since May. So far, September was turning out to be one of the wettest ever.

'Who are the Martyrs when they're at home?' asked Fred, looking a little puzzled. 'I could do with a bit of sunshine myself. Australia will do nicely!'

'He's only joking, Fred,' I tried to explain, as it was obvious that he hadn't a clue who they were.

The Martyrs, or the Tollpuddle Martyrs as they were known, came from Tollpuddle, a small village in Dorset. The age of mechanisation was underway, creating a surplus of labour; an ideal opportunity for unscrupulous landowners to cut wages.

The wages of an agricultural worker in the 1830s were only nine shillings a week. Their pay had been cut several times and was down to six shillings a week, a point where they could barely afford to live. In desperation, the men of Tollpuddle banded together to form the Friendly Society of Agricultural Labourers, the beginning of trade unionism in England.

They refused to work for less than ten shillings a week. In those days, to go before your masters and make such a demand was a brave move because the estate provided not only your entire income, but also shelter for your family. In 1834, six of them were arrested, put on trial and charged under the Unlawful Oaths Act of 1797. They were sentenced to serve seven years in a penal colony in Australia. They all survived and became famous throughout the world, but only one ever returned to the village.

'I take it you're having a bad day then, Woofy?' I enquired.

'It's bad, and it's getting worse by the minute being in here with you two,' he scowled. 'I've had my head stuck down a manhole for the last hour, trying to unblock a drain over at the east wing. On top of that, I've had to show the new houseman around.'

'What's he like then?'

'Gormless – absolutely gormless. He's supposed to be experienced, but I have my doubts. I asked him if he could prepare game. He said he could, so I gave him two rabbits to get ready for Mrs Fleetwood. When I came back sometime later, guess what?' He paused for a moment, trying desperately not to be nice. He'd been at boiling point, but now as the pressure eased, there was a hint of a smile. 'Go on then, tell us!' said Fred.

Woofy couldn't contain himself any longer, and screamed out; 'He was only plucking the bloody things!' I nearly fell off my chair laughing, but Fred just sat there; a sly smirk on his face, I knew he was ready to hit Woofy with some sarcastic remark. 'You don't pluck rabbits then, Woofy?'

He glared at Fred's grinning face and I knew all my peacemaking efforts were about to go out of the window and possibly Fred with them.

Woofy finally blew his top and went into a rage. 'Are you stupid or are you as gormless as he is? Well, I think the answer's both.' Woofy was fuming, as a wet boot went flying across the room, sending Fred diving for the cover of the grass cart. There was no harm done, and he eventually cooled off. For me it had brightened up a miserable morning, and left me with yet another moment to file away in my memory in the box labelled 'happy'.

'If I ever write a book, Woofy, I shall dedicate it to you – to you and the Martyrs.'

'Well I hope it'll have a happy ending,' he said.

There were still many more stories to come from Woofy and Fred. A few more years of fond memories and laughter; laughter that was to follow me through the decades.

Their story came to an end some years ago, and as far as I know, they both led happy and contented lives.

The summer of 1976 had been one of mixed fortunes for me, as I was still struggling to establish a new business. The dry summer didn't help, but at least we were going in the right direction and faced the future with a reasonable amount of optimism. Things could have turned differently ten years earlier, when I first ventured into the wonderful world of the garden. My first day almost turned out to be my last.

2

Derbyshire; A Gardener's Delight

Autumn, 1966

The situation was desperate; I had to get help and fast. The boss was in the greenhouse when I ran in and blurted out; 'THE COWS ARE IN THE GARDEN!' He gave out a strange noise, something like a duck being strangled, and then he was gone, off down the garden like a rocket. We arrived to a scene of devastation. The once-manicured lawns now looked like a rugby field, the black and white devils now busily munching and crunching their way through the flowerbeds, oblivious to the carnage they had caused.

'What happened?' he asked. I had no excuse; on my very last trip across the field, I'd forgotten to close the gate. We stood in silence, a distant church bell ringing out five o'clock. To me, it was the toll of doom – not only signalling the end of the day, but also the end of my job.

It had all been so promising. Just a few hours earlier I'd been full of confidence and enthusiasm, looking forward to a new career and the challenges ahead. Even the journey to work had made it all worthwhile. It was a far cry from the week before, travelling on board a packed, smoke-filled bus, full of people coughing and spluttering on their Woodbines, wheezing and moaning their way into the industrial heart of the city, where any attempt to open a window for a breath of fresh air would be met with enough screaming and cursing to turn the air blue.

With clear skies and a slight chill in the air, my journey to work that morning had been through the beautiful Derbyshire countryside, along quiet country lanes, passing through small villages and places I never knew existed, making our way over the county border and into Staffordshire, where at the top of a hill, an ancient and spooky-looking house came into view; Marchington Hall. There, in those delightful gardens, I was to get my first taste of gardening and life in the great outdoors.

It had been a perfect start and under the boss's watchful eye, I was eager and ready to give it my best shot. 'Something simple to start with,' he said, 'and as a rule, if you are not sure what it is, don't pull it out. First, I'll show you around.' We passed a classy-looking Jensen Interceptor parked up in the yard. 'That car is GT class and hand-built!' said the boss. We made our way through a door and into the gardens. Apart from the local park, it was the biggest garden I'd ever seen. We passed greenhouses, potting sheds, then went onto a wide expanse of lawn surrounded by flowerbeds and shrubberies, making our way to a field at the bottom of the garden.

'I'll show were to put the rubbish,' he said. He asked if I was OK with cows. 'There's a herd of them in this field and they can be a bit nosey. If they're blocking the gate just shout and wave your arms about, they'll soon move back.' There they were, a herd of black and white Friesians, already licking their lips, gazing longingly at the lush green lawns, just out of reach on the other side of the gate. The boss assured me they were harmless, so we pushed them back and made our way through the gate and over to a small dell about thirty yards across the field. 'Put it down there, and make sure you push it well down or they'll eat it,' he warned, 'and be sure to close the gate behind you. I'm mowing the lawns, and if they get scent of fresh grass, they'll be in!'

So began my first day. With the warm September sun on my back and only the sights and sounds of the countryside for company, I began to clear the old summer plants from the beds and borders, digging them over and generally preparing the garden for the winter.

I now had a real sense of freedom; working in the gardens of Marchington Hall seemed like paradise. To be able to look up at the sky and feel the breeze in my face was a pleasure in itself, I was in my element and loved every minute of it. It was a world away from the dark depressing factory I'd left just a few days earlier. That old Victorian building, devoid of natural light, where the only chance of seeing the sun or grabbing a breath of fresh air was out in the yard at break times. Even the canteen with its stale and smoky air was a place to be avoided, but many chose to pass their time there, happily puffing themselves into an early grave. Some had spent their lives in that dismal place, working in an atmosphere of constant noise. The din of countless saws, drills and woodworking machines whined away all day long. From eight o'clock onwards, sign language and lip reading became the norm. Not to mention the smell of paint, varnish and dust that always hung in the air. The days seemed never-ending.

I stood back to look at my work. It was the end of the day and I was pleased with my efforts; the time had passed so quickly. With all the beds and borders neatly dug over and the lawns edged, I was convinced I'd made a good impression on my new boss. I loaded the barrow for last time, ready for the final trip to the dell. As usual, the cattle had gathered around the gate, as they had done all day, but by now I was used to the situation and had no trouble driving them back up the field. Unlike the morning, when it took a few nervous attempts before I could shoo them away. In went the last load and I secured the gate for the last time. I made my way back up the garden path ready for home. Then I remembered the boss's words; 'Make sure you push it well down or the cows will eat it.' I'd forgotten! Grabbing my fork, I dashed back to finish the job. I didn't want to upset him this late in the day by not doing the job properly.

The job was almost done when I heard a rumbling noise behind me. It was the cows; the whole herd was on the move, stampeding down the field, heading towards the gate – and it was open. In my haste, I'd forgotten to close it. I thought cows were supposed to be dumb – not these devils! They had a scent of new-mown grass in their nostrils, and they were determined to get at it. Never in my life have I moved so fast. After sprinting across that field I almost cut them off, but not before about half a dozen or so had made it into the garden and onto the lawns.

'There's no need to panic, you can handle this,' I said to myself, 'the boss need never know.' It was a fateful decision. The ones in the garden were quite calm and settled and apart from a few heavy hoof prints, there was little damage. I had a plan and the job should have been easy. All I had to do was drive the others away and up the field, then open the gate and get the others back on the right side of the fence. That was simple enough. With the main herd out of the way, I returned to the garden to find the others happily munching away, pleased with themselves. I began the job of clearing them from the garden.

It was all going quite well, until they neared the gate. The main herd, who were obviously extremely jealous of their sisters' good fortune, were determined to get their share of that prized fodder. They had already started to move slowly back down the field, but as soon as they saw me open the gate, it was like the January sales at the farmyard and these ladies didn't hold back. They came charging down the field heading towards the gate, headlong into the ones coming out.

Plan A didn't work. There was only one thing left to do. Panic!

I took my life in my hands and made a desperate attempt to stop them by shouting and waving my arms in the air, just as the boss had told me to do that morning. It seemed to do the trick. They came to a grinding halt just short of the gate. Unfortunately, all that waving, shouting and jumping about spooked the ones already in the garden, with predictable results. All hell broke loose; they went into frenzy and took off up the garden heading towards the flowerbeds, leaping and kicking their legs in the air. It was like something out of a Wild West show. The

harder I tried, the more agitated they became. My attempts to resolve the situation myself had been a disaster. That distant church bell now turned into a siren, and it was calling me back to the factory.

The boss was deep in thought, trying to figure out the next course of action. It would be another week before our next visit, so it was decided that urgent repairs had to be done immediately. He went up to the house to explain the situation, while I fetched a barrow full of sharp sand and a couple of forks. We then set about repairing the damage. A time-consuming job that involved lifting each hoofmark with a fork and then filling the gap underneath with sand; some of them were inches deep. After a couple of hours we'd made a reasonable job, and headed for home.

Little was said on the way other than my attempts to apologise and to offer to pay for the damage out of my wages. 'What wages?' came the disheartening reply. To make matters worse, on the way back we had to pick up Cyril and John. They had been working at Mrs Wright's place, a large country house in the village of Ednaston. They had been there since first light, and must have been wondering what had become of us. I'd only met them briefly that morning. Cyril was an old hand, and not far off retirement. He'd spent all his life outdoors as a groundsman. Small and bald with a weather-beaten face, he had a toothless cheeky grin. He seemed a good-natured man and offered help and advice, but as I was to find out later and almost to my cost, Cyril had no time for sarcasm or mickey-takers. Whilst his career was coming to an end, mine was just beginning – or so I had thought. Now I wasn't so sure. John on the other hand was a new recruit like me; starting out, with little experience, but willing to learn.

The boss, Cyril and John stood huddled in the corner of the tool shed, obviously talking about my escapades with the cattle. The look on their faces said it all, and my heart sank further still when I heard the boss say; 'Well Cyril? What shall we do with him?' There was a long pause. Cyril looked me up and down, shaking his head in disapproval, his face deadly serious.

He looked at the boss again, then back at me and shouted 'Sack him!' I was shocked and feared the worst; I was resigned to my fate. Then his eyes began to twinkle and his face lit up, and with that big toothless grin he said; 'We don't want cowboys on the job, do we now?' This seemed to put a smile back on our faces, especially mine, as we headed for home. Still unsure of my future, I was trying desperately to think of something to say. My mind drifted back a couple of weeks to the interview when I first met the boss.

'I'm Mick,' he said as he walked into the room. Freddy was right; he did look just like 'Big Fry' off the television, or to give him his proper name, George Lazenby, the actor who later went on to play James Bond. Before he was famous, he appeared in a TV advert for a Fry's chocolate bar. Mick was a dead ringer for him. Tall and dark with a flashing white smile. His eyes half closed, from long days in the sun, his long dark sideburns giving him that rugged outdoor look. He wouldn't have looked out of place in a Western. Then he took his hat off. He was almost bald, which seriously diminished his Hollywood potential

'I'll be brief,' he said, 'how much do you earn in the factory?' 'Well, give or take a bob or two, around eight pounds a week.' 'I can only pay you six, but there's plenty of overtime.' 'That's OK,' I told him, 'money isn't everything.' At the time I would have paid him just to get away from that dead-end job. 'All I want to know for now is, can you work? The work is hard and the hours are long, and we're out in all weathers. We spend a lot of our time up in the Derbyshire hills – it can be bitterly cold in the winter months. But if you take to it, you will find working outdoors gets into your blood. It can also be very rewarding. What do you think?' 'Is that it?' That's what I'm thinking. 'This must be the shortest interview on record.'

'Well, err, yes!' I said, a little taken aback by the speed and directness of his questions; he certainly didn't hang about. 'The hard work's no problem, I've done a few gardens for neighbours in the past, and I love being outdoors.' Then, trying to impress and show myself as a keen gardener, I added, 'I always watch the gardening programmes on the telly.' This didn't go down well at all. 'I hope you don't think it's a collar and tie job like that Percy Thrower, and you certainly won't have time to smoke a pipe,' he snapped.

Percy Thrower was one of the first celebrity gardeners. With his trademark pipe, he was a household name at the time. He came from the old school of gardeners, back in the days when the head gardener was a man of status and respect, and dressed accordingly. They always wore a collar and tie, and only removed their jacket on the hottest of days.

'That's it then,' he said. 'I'll pick you up a week on Monday,' and he was off. He was right – working outdoors does get into your blood. But he forgot to mention one other vital ingredient that would always be present in the years to come: laughter.

The hour was late when we eventually arrived back in town. Mick assured Cyril and John that they would be paid overtime. This made me feel even worse. Now I would have to pay for their lost time out of my wages, as well as the cattle damage. That is if I had any wages at all – if I had a job at all. Thinking back to the interview and what Mick said about long hours, I decided a little bit of humour might do the trick. I waited until we got out of the van, then I said; 'Mick, I know you said it was going to be long hours but…' 'But don't push your luck,' he said, stopping me in mid-sentence, and then to my relief continued; 'I'll see you in the morning.'

The next few days were spent around the Derbyshire/Staffordshire border, working in a variety of quaint cottage gardens in the villages of Doveridge, Church Broughton and Boyleston. Over at Somersal Herbert, our services were required at the hall. This impressive timber-framed Elizabethan building dated back to 1564. The gardens were in need of a tidy-up ready for some special family occasion. This time, Cyril and John came along to give us a hand.

It was like travelling back in time to a corner of old England, a feeling I'd get many times over the following years, working in gardens steeped in history and tradition. The hall and gardens seemed to be in harmony with the countryside around, and with the first tints of autumn beginning to appear, this English country garden was the perfect place to be. Semi-wild in parts, the gardens had been well maintained so our work was relatively simple; just a case of mowing, edging, and generally sharpening things up.

Everywhere we went, people made us welcome, and there was always tea and biscuits. Unlike the factory, where dear old Dot, the deaf tea lady, would come around at ten o'clock prompt, and serve up a cuppa which had to be drunk at the workbench. If you were unfortunate enough to be at the end of her round, your brew would often be cold and full of dust. Dot had been at the factory since the year dot, obviously causing her to go deaf. Now, our morning tea was something to look forward to, civilised and quaint, typically English, with an endless variety of goodies. The hall was no exception. We all looked forward to the usual refreshments at break times, normally supplied by the house staff, but on one occasion, it was the lady of the house herself, who ordered us all to go over to the outbuildings to await its arrival. 'I hope this will be enough!' she said, smiling, as she and the housemaid set out several trays piled high with sandwiches of every description. 'We wouldn't want you to starve now, would we?' she added, as they made their way back to the house. It was all a bit odd, to say the least.

'What's this all about?' said Mick. We sat there staring at the mountain of food that lay before us, then looking at each other, trying to work out what the hell was going on. Then it all came out. 'It's my fault,' said John, who was looking a little sheepish. 'I left my sandwich box out at break time, and the hounds came in and gobbled up my snap. I was annoyed, so I went over to the house and told them so. "Your dogs have eaten my dinner, missus", I said, "what are you going to do about it?" The maid never said anything, so I thought no more about it.' 'You should

19

have told us,' said Mick, 'we'd have given you some of ours. This is so embarrassing. There's enough food here to feed an army. They must have thought you were some starving wretch off the street in need of a good meal!'

It had certainly been an interesting few days. No words can describe how happy I felt; a new life was opening up for me and I was enjoying myself immensely, relieved I was still in a job after my disastrous start at Marchington.

Coming over the brow of Shaw Wood Hill, the town of Ashbourne is spread out before you. Set in the beautiful Henmore Valley, it sits on the southern edge of the Derbyshire Peak District, the distant peaks indicate a marked change in the landscape. We were now leaving the gentle rolling meadows and hedgerows of the Derbyshire I knew to enter a more wild and rugged – but just as beautiful – landscape. Ashbourne is one of the loveliest of towns, a timeless place. Sitting at the foot of the Peak District, parts of the town have changed little over the centuries. It is the gateway to one of England's great beauty spots at Dovedale.

The boss had certainly done his homework when he chose this prosperous market town as the centre of operations for his new business. A place and people I'd get to know well over the coming years. The town was the perfect place for a small garden service. Prosperous and affluent, it had a thriving agricultural centre. With many other small businesses in the town including numerous light industries, and with the Nestlé factory being one of the largest milk condenseries in Britain, there always seemed to be the sweet smell of success hanging in the air over Ashbourne.

There was no shortage of the type of customer Mick was looking for. Professional and business people, retired people or just plain busy people, people who had no time or inclination to do their own gardens, but had the means to employ someone to do it for them, from just a couple of hours to a full day. If they could pay five shillings an hour, the job was done.

People like the Rev. F.J.H. Lisemore. He lived in the vicarage on Belle Vue Road overlooking St Oswald's Church. 'He's a man

20

you can talk to,' said the boss. 'Remarkably down to earth, for someone so close to heaven.'

No visit to the Reverend's garden would be complete without some interesting conversation about his work. He would enthuse about his beloved church, his half-lit pipe darting about in the air, trying to point out to us some interesting pieces of architecture or carving on its glorious tower and elegant spire. 'At 212 feet, it is without doubt one of the finest in England!' he would say.

Windmill Lane on the north side of the town has many fine residential houses. The owners of some of Ashbourne's oldest businesses lived there. Mr Callow, always immaculately dressed, as you would expect from the man who ran the family clothing shops in the town, famous for clothes since the nineteenth century. The Pearsons, who ran the famous gingerbread shop on St John's Street, also lived on the lane and, like the Callows, had been in the town for generations.

The gardens of Windmill Lane were typical English gardens, informal and unsophisticated, created by their owners to reflect their own individual styles and tastes. You could see they had been loved and well looked after over the years. Some of the older residents now sought help from the likes of us with some of the heavy work, such as hedge cutting or digging over the vegetable patch.

Nearly all were keen gardeners, and knew what they were talking about. This made me realise just how little knowledge I had when it came to the technicalities of gardening, especially in the botanical names department. One lady gardener in particular was a real irritating smart Alec who always loved to show off, calling all the plants in her garden by their botanical names. She knew that I'd only just started in the job, but still asked me to clear the leaves from under the acer pseudoplatanus. She could have been talking double Dutch for all I knew. Determined not to show my ignorance I promised to do it, then ran off to find the boss and garbled out 'Where the hell is the acersudoduckplatypus or whatever it is', only to find out it was a sycamore tree at the bottom of the garden. Mick found my tongue-twisting interpretation hilarious, and told me not worry – after all, there are only several hundred plant families to learn about. 'Is that all?' I said. 'That's no problem.' 'Good,' he said, 'because after that you will have several hundred thousand different species to get your head around. It will come with experience! You'll learn your trade hands-on in the field. The time for books and studying will come later.' He was right; it seemed a daunting prospect ahead of me, but in Mick I had an excellent teacher.

We moved on to Thorpe, a grey-stoned village that lies at the southern entrance to Dovedale, rightly described as one of the most picturesque places in the land. Although Thorpe was only a few miles from Ashbourne, the gardens were different. More of the cottage type, with boundaries of grey-stoned walls rather than hedges. The landscape was dramatic, but not as quiet as you might think. Every now and then a low-flying jet fighter would scream over our heads, frightening the living daylights out of us. To see them streak down the valleys and actually be looking down on them was a remarkable sight. We looked after several gardens in the village, including Thorpe Grange, home of the Metcalfes and their dog, Gear; an apt named for an engineer's pet. Their garden offered splendid views across open fields to the grey-capped hill of the famous Thorpe Cloud.

Alsop-en-le-Dale is mentioned in the Doomsday Book. It lies in a quiet, secluded valley five miles north of Ashbourne. The hall dates back to the sixteenth century, its charming gardens seeming to have stepped out of the pages of history, along with the gardener. One of the flat cap and whippet brigade, he wouldn't have looked out of place in Queen Victoria's England. His age, heavy clothes and ample waistline disguised a surprisingly fit and active man, showing us cocky lads from the city how digging should be done. His spade had a heavy wooden handle, but the blade was sharp and polished from years of use. We were young and fit but we couldn't keep up with him, he must have had cast iron back muscles; he was relentless, like a human rotavator. I am in no doubt that John and I would have been dug in with the rest of the muck if we'd stayed around much longer.

I ended the week with a plateful of leftovers whizzing past my nose. Colonel Waldron was Mick's solicitor, a flamboyant and jovial character. When I first met him, he opened a window to throw out the remains of the family breakfast on to the rose bed where I was working. 'Oops, I'm sorry,' he said, and then with a wink, he turned to his wife and said; 'Look, dear, even the birds won't eat your cooking.' What a week it had been. I couldn't believe how many gardens I'd been to, and the people I'd met, but we were moving on again. The next couple of weeks would see us doing something totally different.

We were called in to help out at the golf course, a mile and a half outside Ashbourne, near the village of Clifton. With its elevated position, working on the course made a pleasant change to the usual routine. Its picturesque location offered splendid views across to Dovedale and the Peak District. The club was without a resident green keeper. Our work involved some maintenance on the putting greens, as well as creating some new tees. In Cyril, we had just the man for the job. With all his years of experience as a groundsman, Cyril took charge of the whole operation, including the use of the club's tractor. Although Cyril didn't hold a licence to drive on the road, he knew that old tractor like the back of his hand; he'd driven them for years on golf courses and sports fields up and down the country. He was confident it would get the job done.

With business on the up, there was another new recruit, Darren. On his first day on the job, he was to be under Cyril's wing, and just like mine, his first day would turn out to be one he wouldn't forget in a hurry. Cyril's first encounter with the old tractor didn't go as planned. The tractor shed was at the top end of the course, on the side of a hill. Unfortunately for Cyril he forgot to take into account the steep terrain. When he came shooting out of the shed, losing control, he headed off down the course at speed. To make matters worse, there was a small two-

wheeled trailer attached with Darren sitting in the back, as they sped on down the hill towards the main road. Cyril had no choice but to hit the brakes, with the predictable results. Long strips of turf were ripped up as he tried desperately to slow the machine down, but it continued on its way down the hill and across the fairways. As well as being steep, the course was also uneven; this caused the trailer to shake violently, detaching it from the tractor. Cyril finally reached level ground and managed to reduce speed, only to see the trailer come flying past. It was like a scene from *Ben-Hur*, Darren was hanging on to that horseless chariot for dear life, his long hair flowing in the wind, speeding onwards heading towards the hedge that separated the course from the Clifton road and what seemed certain disaster. Luckily it overturned just before impact, throwing him clear of the trailer, sending him skidding across the turf on his backside.

The rest of us, who had been watching the drama unfold, came running down the hill to help. Darren was already on his feet and grinning, none the worse for his ordeal. If anything, he seemed to be a little amused by it all. Cyril on the other hand was in shock. Looking back up the course, the damage was considerable; almost in tears, he was inconsolable. The boss, as usual, took it all in his stride, thankful no one had been hurt. His view was that damage could always be repaired.

The membership played on around us. It was obvious what they thought about contractors. With black looks, snide comments and golf balls flying all around us, we set about repairing the damage. By the end of the day it didn't look too bad. Cyril had cheered up a little and was almost back to his old self. The boss had flatly refused his offer to pay for the damages. We put our tools away and made ready for home.

Then came one of those moments we've all had, of opening your mouth before putting your brain in gear. Something you've said, then instantly regretted it, like my attempt to put a smile back on Cyril's face with some ill-chosen words of sympathy. Remembering Cyril's comments about 'cowboys' after my disaster

at Marchington, and how it had cheered me up, I thought I'd try some of the same, a little humour to make him feel better. I cracked a joke about his driving skills. It was a big mistake. I've never been any good at telling jokes, and I got it all wrong. A garden fork was instantly thrust against my face. With one of the prongs almost up my nose, Cyril's eyes blazed with rage. 'Next time it'll be up a darker place than this,' he snarled, 'you're nothing but a novice.' For a few seconds there was an embarrassing silence, a look of shock on everyone's face. Darren sat there wide-eyed, wondering what sort of outfit he'd joined. I kept silent; no words of apology would be enough. Cyril had been humiliated by a smart-arse kid who knew nothing, and he made dammed sure it wouldn't happen again.

Cyril was right, I had only been in the job five minutes, and compared to his vast experience I had a lot to learn. I was nothing but a novice.

3

Kedleston Hall

Not far from Derby lies the village of Kedleston, home to the Curzons, a family who came over with William the Conqueror. Passing through the North Lodge into their estate, the majestic Kedleston Hall, I seemed to have entered another world, a place of peace and tranquillity, an oasis of quiet in a modern world.

Marchington had been impressive, but nothing could prepare me for the magnificent building I was about to see. We drove through lovely parkland down an avenue of trees, some of them ancient. One massive oak lay on its side, a victim of recent storms. The approach to the hall gave the visitor a feeling of expectation, almost of mystery about what lay beyond the distant trees. After half a mile the woodland began to thin and the first tantalising glimpse of the hall, still half hidden in the trees, came into view. Suddenly, we were in open meadow and there it was – the great house.

Set in beautiful countryside, it was bathed in the morning sun. Several lakes gave the impression of a river winding its way through the great estate. With a backdrop of trees on the distant hills in their autumn colours, it seemed picture perfect.

We stopped for a while. 'I always like to take a few minutes if I can,' said Mick, 'and it's a great place for wildlife.' I could see his point; the lakes were alive with wildfowl of every description. Herons sat motionless at the water's edge, while a squadron of wild geese came in from the north, circling and splashing down in a great commotion close to a tree-covered island, dense with impenetrable undergrowth.

'Well, they certainly picked the right spot to build this place!' I said, believing the landscape before me was natural, but I was wrong. Mick told me it was all man-made. The lakes had been created from a small stream, the Cutler Brook, which runs through the estate. 'Believe it or not,' he said, 'it was all dug out by hand, with pick and shovel, and moved by horse and cart.' The hall was built over 200 years ago by the first Baron Scarsdale. He even had the village moved a mile to the west, so as not to detract from the splendour of his new house.

The drive led us down to a beautiful bridge, with cascades flowing into a lower lake below, and then on past a small church, all that remained of the original village. We entered the stabling area, the red brick buildings in stark contrast to the hall with its ornate sandstone splendour.

I'd come to Kedleston for a few days to give a hand with the autumn clean-up. 'Old Tom should be over there,' said Mick, pointing to a dark and dingy gardener's shed in the corner of the yard. 'He'll show you what to do, and I'll see you tonight.' Dressed in a blue boiler suit, flat cap and wellies, Tommy Brown was waiting. He seemed a little agitated.

'Hello, Tom, I'm George. I've come to give you a hand with the...' 'What time do you call this?' He nearly bit my head off. I had no chance to introduce myself. 'You should have been here at eight!' he snapped. It was barely five past.

'Well, you can't do the leaves today, the cavalry's out. Grab a rake and a wheelbarrow, and I'll get you to clear some dead wood.' I took a rake down off the rack. 'Not that one – it's mine!' he shouted. I grabbed a wheelbarrow. 'Not that one, it's...' 'Let me guess – it's yours, Tom.' He looked daggers at me. It wasn't a good start, but I'd learnt one thing already; you needed to be a mind reader to work at this place.

We set off towards the garden with me pushing an antiquated wooden wheelbarrow, rattling across a cobbled yard. It must have been there since Victorian times; even empty it took some pushing. We were joined by the gardener, Ken Woof. He was polite enough, but Tom didn't want to know. Not a word was said, none of the usual introductions of people meeting for the first time. He seemed to have taken an instant dislike to me. We passed through an ancient oak door studded with nails, where the initials 'N.C. 1680' had been hammered in centuries ago by Nathaniel Curzon. This led us to a swimming pool area surrounded by pergolas. Roses, clematis and honeysuckle covered its stone pillars and oak beams. We looked out onto a wide expanse of lawn. This was my first glimpse of the gardens of Kedleston and I had a feeling about the place; it was pleasing to the eye, and hopefully an interesting and enjoyable place to work. Tom pointed to a large stone and glass building at the far end of the lawn. 'That's the orangery,' he said, 'there's a lot of dead wood lying around. It came down in the storms. Pile it up, and I'll pick it up later.' That was the last I saw of them.

Around mid morning, I could hear the distant sound of guns. Perhaps it was the cavalry, thinking back to what Tom had said earlier. It was a strange feeling. I was completely alone. The place seemed to be deserted. As well as the orangery, there was a sunken rose garden and a hexagonal-shaped summerhouse with a table and chairs inside – the ideal place to eat, out of Tom's way. After lunch I explored the rest of the gardens. The south front of the hall was almost as impressive as the north, with a large expanse of lawn that seemed to stretch all the way up to the trees at the top of the hill. Crossing the lawn, I discovered there was an invisible barrier, a wall that seemed to circle the whole of the gardens, with a drop of several feet into the meadow below. This, I was to learn, was called a 'ha-ha'. It's what people say when they come across it.

By late afternoon, the guns were silent and it was time for home. Back in the yard, I saw Tom disappearing under the archway, his barrow full of rubbish, on his way to the tip. I could see he'd been sweeping the leaves out of the garages. This would be a good opportunity to talk to him again, to try and get into his good books. So as a surprise I decided to finish the job for him. With the floors clean, and the rubbish left in a neat pile, I awaited Tom's return. Expecting gratitude, what I got was quite the opposite. 'What you have done that for?' he said, shouting at the top of his voice and kicking the leaves all over the floor. Tom was hopping mad, literally. He walked with a limp, and the sight of him hopping and skipping around the floor like some demented Morris dancer, trying to kick the leaves in the air, was one of the funniest things I've ever seen. Then, like some lunatic, he started sweeping them up again, while nervously peeping around the door. 'This blokes a nutter,' I thought to myself. 'Quick!' he said. 'He's here, grab a brush and start sweeping.' Now he'd really lost it. I feared for my safety. Just then a mud-spattered Land Rover turned into the yard. Out stepped an elderly gentleman. He seemed to be a friend, and about the same age as Tom. 'I see you have a new assistant, Tom,' he said. 'Yes, it's what's-his-name from that gardening firm,' replied Tom. He'd forgotten my name already, so I stepped in. 'Hello mate, the name's...' Before I could say another word, Tom was in my face again, shouting his head off. 'It's Lord Scarsdale to you, me lad, not mate.' Oops, I'd forgotten to read Tom's mind again. 'Sorry ma... I mean your Lordship,' I said, nearly repeating myself. 'Is Tom looking after you?' he enquired. I assured him everything was fine, and he was on his way.

'Seems a nice bloke,' I said. Tom reared up again. 'He's not a bloke, he's a lord, and just you remember it. And there's another thing, next time ask me before you start doing my work.' 'I was only trying to help, Tom,' I said sharply. I was now feeling a little brassed off at his attitude. 'Well, maybe,' he shrugged, calming down a little. 'I like to leave something to do, even if there's nothing to do. It keeps me happy. It also makes them happy to see you busy doing something. Even when there's nothing to do!' Now I was sure he was bonkers.

On the way home, Mick asked how the day had gone. I'd found it really interesting, but the place seemed deserted, apart from old misery-guts Tom and his mate Woof, there was no one

else around. 'Tom's from a different age,' he said. 'He's lived and worked on the estate all his life, and seen many changes. The time of the great estates passed decades ago. And what you see today is only a shadow of what used to be. People like Tom are the last of a generation. When he started work as a young man in the twenties, there would have been an army of gardeners and estate men, earning no more than two pounds a week. Although he's retired, he probably looks on us as a threat to his livelihood – which isn't true, of course.'

'What about the cavalry? Tom said I couldn't do the leaves because the cavalry was out. I could hear the guns, but there was no sign of the cavalry all day!' Mick smiled. 'The guns you could hear was the shoot. That's why the place was so quiet. All the men were out in the woods, beating. The "cavalry" Tom was talking about was the leaves – it's impossible to rake them up on a windy day, you must have seen them blowing across the lawns. "No raking today, the cavalry's out!" It's an old saying.' I watched the cavalry for the next couple of days, great swarms of beech and oak leaves, whipped up by the wind charging across the gardens like a multicoloured cavalry shining in the sun.

I spent most of my time alone, which I didn't mind – it was a lovely place to work. One day I heard a curious sound coming from the direction of the east wing. Like a distant steam train whistle, getting louder and longer the closer it came. 'Wooof, Wooooof, Wooouooooof!' It echoed all around the grounds. A lady appeared looking for Woofy. He had been working some distance away with Tommy Brown. He arrived, breathless, to answer her call. After puffing and panting his apologies for being late, he was immediately set upon by a beady-eyed bull terrier. The exhausted gardener had to dance a silly jig all around her trying to avoid the little beast who was snapping and snarling at his feet. Watching from a distance, I found the whole spectacle hilarious, until it headed across the lawns in my direction. 'He won't hurt you!' she cried, puffing away on a long cigarette holder. 'He's only playing,' she said as the bloody thing gnawed away at my ankles and boots. Now it was my turn to be doing a silly jig around her Ladyship, the second Viscountess Scarsdale.

Lady Ottilie didn't stand on ceremony; she said what she thought. We all received an ear-bashing at one time or another, usually for some minor misdemeanour. She once threatened to send us all back to Butlins when she found us sunbathing on the lawns with our shirts off. 'Where do you think you are? A holiday camp? Get those shirts on, and get out of sight. Visitors come here for a pleasant day out, not to be frightened to death by you lot!' she stormed. Despite her Vesuvius-like tendencies, we all liked her, especially young John with his less than formal greetings of 'Hey up Mrs Scarsdale, how's ya doin?' or 'Mornin' missus, how's the old man today?' Her face would light up in great amusement, much to the disgust of Tommy Brown, who would cringe in his boots. She could be quite emotional, shedding tears of sorrow for a nest of partridges she'd been protecting, mistakenly mangled by a lawnmower. Then tears of rage, as Dozy Dick, the part time gardener, chopped off her beloved daffodils too early.

Benny was always at her side, on the lookout for some unsuspecting victim. 'One of these days I'm going to swing for that dog!' said Woofy. 'The trouble is he's a cunning bugger, and only attacks when she's around.' Benny the bull terrier, or bull terrible as we called him, was anything but brave. If he came across you alone and without the back up of his mistress, he would turn tail and run. Only with his great protector around would he launch his attack, smug in the knowledge he would be safe from a kick up the backside. But Benny wasn't as clever has he thought and one day, much to the delight of Woofy, he made a big mistake.

We'd been working in the rose garden. Benny suddenly appeared from behind the yew hedge, no doubt preparing for a sneaky attack. As soon as he saw us he stopped dead in his tracks. 'Watch out, Woofy, Benny's here, her Ladyship must be on her way.' 'I don't think so,' he said. 'She's away, that little sod shouldn't be out!' Benny had escaped. Pleased with his new-found freedom, he stood there for a few moments thinking, looking back, waiting for his Ladyship to arrive. It didn't take long for his little brain to work out he had made a mistake, and was in a sticky situation. As predicted, Benny turned tail and skedaddled back to the hall as fast as his little legs could carry him. Woofy's face lit up – now was his chance for revenge. 'Right, you little ****' he cried, taking off in hot pursuit. I called after him, begging him not to do anything stupid. 'Don't worry,' he said. 'It'll be anything but stupid!' I followed on, a little concerned by Woofy's intentions. Benny was sometimes kept in a small yard adjacent the church and it was to there he made his retreat to find sanctuary from Woofy, but that was another big mistake on Benny's part. He was now trapped. The assault had already begun when I arrived. Benny cowered in the corner of the yard yelping and whimpering. Thankfully, and to my relief, a good soaking was all he had to endure. Administered by Woofy in sweet revenge. I asked Woofy about the next time. 'There won't be a next time,' he said. 'I've had my satisfaction, and that's good enough for me.' 'No, I mean the next time Benny's about with her Ladyship, and he sees you.' There was no comment.

Autumn was giving way to winter, and the nature of the work was changing. Lawnmowers were being serviced and put away. Planting and pruning became the order of the day. At Kedleston, thousands of new trees were to be planted, creating several new plantations in various parts of the estate. Our firm was to provide the extra labour needed for such a large-scale operation.

The meeting place was in the stabling yard, and on this occasion, we were to be accompanied by Lord Scarsdale himself and Mr Haines, who seemed to be some sort of estate manager. Together, they were going to oversee the whole operation.

I could now see what Mick was talking about when he said the time of the great estate had passed. A handful of men were all the labour the Kedleston estate could muster, with six of us making up the shortfall. His Lordship and Mr Haines stood out from the rest, being smartly dressed in their country attire. We followed them, armed with our spades, forks and shovels, looking like a motley bunch of peasants about to go to war.

Led by his Lordship, Mr Haines and Mr Grumpy (Tommy Brown), who seemed to be a favourite, the planting party set out in a convoy of tractors, trailers and vans, following his Lordship's blue Land Rover across the park. It was mid November, and after a period of damp murky weather, the skies were clear again. With the lakes on fire from the early morning sun, we crossed the Adam Bridge heading towards Ireton Lodge and out of the park to our first destination, the old walled garden.

Now derelict and overgrown, I don't think we'll see the likes of such a splendid facility again. The old walled garden used to be the centre of food production for the estate. It delivered an all-year round supply of fresh fruit and vegetables to the hall's kitchens. It must have been a marvellous sight in years gone by, when fully staffed. From first light, the place would have been buzzing with activity, from young journeymen learning their trade to the head gardener overseeing the whole operation, on whose shoulders rested the success of the gardens, and more importantly the reputation of the house. It now lies in ruins, with just a few sheep grazing inside. There were traces of white paint on the walls, showing evidence of where magnificent hot houses once stood, capable of producing exotic fruits. The remains of a few old fruit trees, plum, pear and apple, once carefully trained against the red brick walls, now stood wild and overgrown.

Its only use now was for storage; a place used by the gamekeepers and estate men.

With all the necessary tools and equipment loaded up, we made our way out of the yard and headed northwest to an area known as Draycotts.

Three old Scots pine trees stood in the middle of Draycotts, tall and stately like cathedral columns. They must have been there for over a century, surveying the land around them. Now they were about to have some company.

The first task was to clear away some fallen branches. This was to be his Lordship's job; he liked to get involved, and was apparently an expert with a chainsaw. With his trusty saw in hand we all gathered around, ready to drag the loose timber away, but there was a problem. It wouldn't start. After several attempts of choke on, choke off, and choke on again, it still wouldn't start.

After refusing all offers of help, his Lordship decided it must be a dirty spark plug. The tool kit was called for. With a clean plug, his Lordship was confident it would start. He set off again, pulling for all he was worth, but to no avail. 'It must be the air filter!' he said, pausing for breath. The air filter was duly cleaned, and he set off again. He was nearly seventy and was becoming tired and irritable. We all stood around, a little embarrassed, not daring to say anything or make any suggestions. Until I opened my big mouth. 'Is there any fuel in it, m'lord?' There was a stunned silence, it took me all of a millisecond for me to realise I'd put my foot in it. Then came his response. To make matters worse, his Lordship sometimes had a little difficulty getting his words out. They seemed to take an age to clear his lips. 'I wo wo wo wouldn't have brought the blo blo bloody th th th thing, if there was no fu fu fu fuel in it, would I, you bloody idiot.' It was time for a quick exit, but I turned only to be looking straight into the eyes of my old pal, Grumpy Brown, who was inches from my face. His eyes were enormous, magnified by the thick lenses of his glasses, with clenched fists and gritted teeth ready to devour me. If looks could kill, I'd have been dead in an instant. His Lordship had to give it up. 'It's a job for the repairers!' he declared. The chainsaw never did start, and we cleared the dead wood by hand and as far as I know, no one ever did check the fuel tank.

Our task was to form a new plantation around the old pines, and after that tense start we set about the job in hand. Working in pairs, the older men began setting out the young trees, while the younger ones followed up, doing the spade work. Planting was easy; the young trees were about a foot high, with a small root system so all that was required was to make a slit in the ground, pop the tree in, and then firm it up, and on to the next.

Mr Haines, a tall, wily ex-military man, kept a close eye on us, the outsiders. A bit too close, as far as I was concerned. Fifty yards into my first row, I stopped for a rest. I turned to see him following behind. In his wake lay the young pines, strewn across the ground. 'What the ...!' was all I could say. 'Not firm enough, do them again!' he muttered, as he walked on by. Cyril told me later that he overheard Mr Grumpy telling Mr Haines to keep an eye on me. It wouldn't be the last time he would come along and have a tug at my row of trees to see if they were firm enough. It was obvious I'd been singled out for some special treatment.

Being one of the highest points on the estate, Draycotts offered excellent views of the hall some two to three miles distant, its lakes shining like silver in the winter sun. With the weather calm and relatively mild for November, the new plantation was one of the most enjoyable of places to work.

Tea breaks were taken in the field. We all gathered around the estate tractor and trailer, getting to know one another. Fred Brown (no relation to Tommy Brown) had been in farming all his life, a typical flat cap and waistcoat man. Handkerchief always in hand, Fred's long, pointy nose had a permanent dewdrop on the end of it.

Jack McGowan was a Korean War veteran. Slightly built, with ginger hair, he always wore a trilby hat. He and his wife Beryl, who was quite formidable and twice his size, lived at Ireton Lodge, the middle one of the three gatehouses on the estate. They didn't drive and only left the estate once a week, taking the bus to town to do the weekly shop at Tesco, but the highlight of their year came with the summer holidays. Then they spent two weeks in Skegness and a week in Burton on Trent. Why Burton, I never found out, but Jack had five good reasons to visit Skegness, and they all began with the letter b; bingo, betting, beer, bed, and Beryl. John Guest drove the estate tractor, and worked alongside Jack. A much younger man, he took a lot of the heavy work off

Jack's shoulders. He lived with his wife in one of the estate cottages in the village.

The weather suddenly changed; gone were the calm sunny days, now we were being battered by gales, torrential rain, sleet and snow. The nature of Draycotts had changed and being on the side of a hill, we were exposed to it all. The rain was almost horizontal, and the wind roared through the tops of the old pines. We had to stay well clear, as they swayed violently, shedding dead wood all around. Mick was right; it could be cold in the winter months and we were having a taste of it, but as bad as it was, there was beauty to be found in that winter weather. Watching those dramatic storm clouds racing across the landscape did add a certain atmosphere to the job, and thankfully it did have one blessing. With the start of the bad weather, we saw the last of Mr Haines.

His Lordship and Fred and Tommy Brown had gone on ahead of us to our next destination; the Wilderness. Their objective was to remove a lower branch from a beech tree. What they thought would be a simple job turned out to be more difficult. Fortunately for Tommy Brown there had been a delay, caused by the three of them arguing about who should volunteer to climb the ladder. It had been decided that the fairest thing to do was that the youngest of the three should do the job. They were all pushing seventy, but it was left to Tommy Brown with his dodgy leg to make the ascent. Luckily, we arrived just in time. Tom was several feet off the ground when I took the saw from his hand. You could see the relief on his face and we even managed to force a smile out of the old sod.

The Wilderness plantation inside the park is long established, with many old deciduous trees. The area had been deliberately left to grow wild and unlike the easy planting of the new pine forest, our work in the Wilderness was hard going. The new trees were all broad leaf, mainly oak and beech, transplanted from the Long Walk, planted at random wherever we could find a space. The going was tough; trying to dig through a thick matt of ancient meadow to the soil below was difficult, back-breaking work.

In bad weather, meal times were taken in the sanctuary of an old hunting lodge close by. Known as the Woodyard, the building was semi-derelict and dated back over 200 years. It was unlike anything we had ever seen before. 'This really is a look back in time,' shouted Mick, as we entered the mill. The noise was deafening. 'Some of this machinery must have been used to build the Ark!' A large circular saw hummed away, driven by wide leather belts and pulleys that rattled across the ceiling. There was little evidence of safety guards or equipment, inches of sawdust on the floor and piles of wood everywhere. We made the best of it. At least we were out of the cold.

Then came a moment that should have been filmed for posterity. Sometime in his life Fred Brown had picked up the gift of the auctioneer, and it was his party piece. Persuaded by his workmates to give us boys from the gardening firm a display of his talents, Fred grabbed a mallet off the bench and took to the floor. Standing a few yards away, with his audience before him, he brought the mallet down, and the sale began.

Pointing to Cyril, he shouted 'Who'll give me a pound for this fine beast?' This brought fits of laughter. A hand went up, the first bid was made and he was off. 'Who'll give me two, three, four?' with hands going up all over the room. With a flash of his hand and a slap of his thigh, Fred confirmed each bid as the tempo increased. His coat flew across the room, then, as if our beloved Benny was on his heels, he began a crazy jig. Pointing, slapping, and raising his knees in the air, it was a hilarious sight. With the bidding at around £500, his words became inaudible, merging into a continuous line of gobbledygook. Unable to understand a word he was saying, the bidding went out of the window, and we began to clap. Fred's performance would have put any modern-day rapper to shame. He reached a breathtaking crescendo and brought the proceedings to a close by selling Cyril to the gentleman on his right, Darren, for the princely sum of two thousand pounds.

Work on the plantations continued for several weeks. Depending on his shooting commitments, Lord Scarsdale would often accompany us – along with his trusty chainsaw of course.

Born in 1898, Richard Curzon became the second Viscount Scarsdale and the twenty-ninth Lord of Kedleston in 1925 following the death of his uncle, Lord Curzon. Even in his late sixties, he was still fit and active. In his younger days he had been a keen amateur boxer, evident in his rugged but still handsome features. In later years he became a respected referee. As Vice President of the British Boxing Board of Control, his knowledge of the sport was immense, and his eyes would light up whenever the subject came up. Always willing to give us his views and opinions on the fighters of the day – Mohamed Ali, Henry Cooper and the up-and-coming Joe Bugner.

Stories abound of his younger days, when he used to carry two pairs of boxing gloves on his travels around the estate. Poachers, if caught, had two choices. Prosecution or a round of boxing with his Lordship, and with poaching being a serious offence, offenders unvaryingly chose the latter.

One story was of a young poacher called Billy. Back in the dark days of unemployment and depression before the Second World War, Billy had been caught poaching by the gamekeepers, and was held until his Lordship arrived. When asked what he was doing on his land Billy replied 'Why is it your land?'

'It's my land because it was given to me by my forefathers, handed down through generations,' explained his Lordship.

'How did they get it?'

'It was given to them by the King.'

'Who gave it to him?'

'No one. He fought for it.'

'Well, and I'll fight you for it then!' said Billy.

Then to his amazement, his Lordship said 'Fair enough, I'll get the gloves.' Ready to administer his own form of punishment by giving Billy a box around the ears, his Lordship was in for a shock. No matter how hard he tried, he couldn't hit him. Billy was useful, very useful; ducking and diving; he blocked every blow his Lordship could throw at him. This went on for a couple of minutes, until Billy realised he was in a hopeless situation, and sooner or later, he would have to take his medicine, and what the alternative would be if he didn't. Billy dropped his guard and took a few blows. His Lordship stopped the contest, demanding to know why Billy had ceased to defend himself. 'A cut lip and a bloody nose are far better than the nick!' he said. As a fellow pugilist, Billy had gained his Lordship's respect. It is said he was offered a job, but declined. Promising never to return, he was allowed to go on his way

Time eventually caught up with the old Woodyard. One day whilst driving the estate tractor and trailer through Kedleston village, the estate men were pulled over. They had been followed by a gentleman, who just happened to be the local health and safety officer. His intention was to lecture Jack McGowan on the dangers of riding on the back of an open trailer. 'What's it got to do with you?' asked Jack, annoyed at the inconvenience. 'Well, it looks like you could do with some advice on safety matters!' he said, demanding to know who their employer was and where they were based. An appointment was made. Apparently, the man was speechless when he entered the old Woodyard for the inspection. It was closed down with immediate effect, until it could be upgraded into the modern world.

With Christmas upon us and the new plantations finished, it was time to move on. Before we left, we were all asked to go over to the estate office, where to our surprise, everyone was handed a brace of pheasants and a brown envelope containing a few pounds from his Lordship, who thanked each and every one of us personally for our efforts, although this did take some time, due to his difficulty with certain words. The occasion was nearly ruined by one of our crew, who whispered under his breath 'At this rate we'll be here till Easter!'

My first winter had given me a taste of just how cold the great outdoors can be, but the discomforts were nothing compared to the pleasures of working in the Derbyshire countryside, in beautiful gardens such as Kedleston, with its history, characters and echoes of the past giving me a glimpse of another world, and times gone by. Many years have passed since the planting party set out on that cold November morning. Today, whenever I pass by the old walled garden and look over towards Draycotts, I think of the old timers who are no longer with us. But the old pines are still there, now barely visible. The young saplings we planted all those years ago are now over forty years old, maturing fast, touching the shoulders of the fully-grown trees.

4

Film Stars, Football and Dashboard Safaris

Spring was just around the corner. A carpet of snowdrops covered the gardens of the Lloyds Bank. This fine stone-fronted building stands alongside the Henmore Brook on Compton Street, Ashbourne.

The walled garden at the rear of the building was rather plain, just a few trees and shrubs, but it did have rich dark soil, enabling the manager to have a good-sized vegetable plot at the bottom of the garden. He normally tended the plot himself, but for one reason or another hadn't got around to doing the winter digging. He was away on holiday, so we thought it would be a nice surprise if we did the job for him.

Cyril and I, together with Darren, who nearly came to grief on the golf course, set to work.

We could hear a lot of activity that afternoon, some sort of commotion in the distance; it seemed to be getting closer as the day wore on. Finally, it was on the other side of the wall, where Henmore Brook ran through the town.

The Shrovetide football game was taking place.

The game is played over two days, between the Up'ards and the Down'ards. The goals are three miles apart, and who you play for depends on which side of the Henmore Brook you live. The whole town takes part.

We'd almost finished when it appeared – a ball, sitting in the middle of our freshly-dug vegetable plot. We were about to see some of the action close up, and as far we were concerned, a little bit too close for comfort.

It must have come over the wall, which was eight to ten feet high at that point, but further down the garden it dropped away, and this is where the first player emerged racing towards the ball, the others following hot on his heels.

The poor fellow did manage to grab it, but only for a second before he was pounced upon by the rest. The few turned into many, and then into a heaving mass. It began to move, pushing and shoving its way around the vegetable plot. Suddenly, it seemed as if the whole of Ashbourne had come to tea. The garden became a battleground, with bodies everywhere, people slipping and sliding in the mud, losing their place and then diving full length back into the pile, their arms and legs disappearing and then reappearing as a ball of human beings moved across the garden, crushing and trampling everything in its path, before spewing out of the garden gates and into the bus station.

We just stood there, looking on in disbelief. What was left was worse than the stampede at Marchington – a scene of utter

devastation, with crushed trees and shrubs. The lovely carpet of snowdrops had completely disappeared and the vegetable plot was as flat as a Shrove Tuesday pancake.

'Well, at least it's ready for turf,' quipped Cyril.

On his return, the manager thanked us for our efforts.

'It's unfortunate that I wasn't here,' he said. 'I could have told you, we never dig anything over until after the game, and now you can see why!'

After a lifetime outdoors, Cyril retired. I had learnt so much from him, and was sorry to see him go. We had our ups and downs, but we parted the best of friends. Cyril's departure opened the door for me, and I was given the opportunity of running my own team. This would of course mean extra responsibility, but also extra money, and most important of all, the use of the works van. At this time, I had recently got married to Kath and we couldn't afford a car of our own, but that old Volkswagen van was as good as a Rolls Royce to us.

It gave us freedom. 'Treat it as your own,' said the boss. So I did, washing it and polishing it. I kept it pretty well immaculate. So did the others. In those days, the works van was your only form of transport, unlike today when everyone has a car. Now the works van is simply a tool to get the job done, to be washed and cleaned once in a blue moon, a place of clutter, almost like a mobile wheelie bin, and a place crawling with wildlife, where life and death struggles are played out every day. Sometimes it's almost like being on a miniature safari – a dashboard safari.

Dawn is usually a quiet time. On entering the van, the first job is to clear a path through the countless cobwebs and spiders blocking your way, and then check the place out for any dead carcasses, especially behind the sun visors, where many of the victims have been dragged into the hunter's lair, leftovers from the previous night's carnage.

Daytime is usually a peaceful time, a time for observation. To watch as gentle butterflies, ladybirds and all manner of weird and wonderful insects fly in and out, but be sure to keep the camp secure. Big cats, if they get the chance, will ransack the place. Today's cats are well fed, and stealing your food is far easier than hunting mice. If you're lucky, you'll get the chance to see new life being born. We once witnessed a wonderful sight one early dawn as hundreds of newly hatched spiders, no bigger than pinheads, descended all around us on silver gossamer threads shining in the morning sun. Like little soldiers, parascending into our hair and clothes, some coming to grief in our tea and coffee. Now free from their birthplace in the roof of the cab, they unhooked their tethers and made a dash for freedom.

Just like the big game reserves in Africa, the best time to see a real dashboard safari is on a moonlit night. That's when it really comes alive.

To spend a night camping in the works van isn't for the faint-hearted.

You think you've done a good job but no matter how clean you think it is, things begin to stir around sunset. Night predators emerge, creeping from behind cracks and crevices, making ready for the night's work.

Fat-bellied spiders spin their webs in the corners of the windscreen in anticipation of a good night's hunting. After dark, the action begins. Most of the little flies and insects stand no chance. After straying into the van during the day, they've been trapped. With nowhere to run, it's only a matter of time before they are caught in a web and devoured.

Then, occasionally, you're woken in the night by the sound of an epic battle taking place. I once watched a giant spider moving swiftly across the ceiling, making his way down the windscreen and on to the dashboard, a killer hunter looking for his next victim.

To the right something moved. Walking slowly around the steering wheel came a large, winged creature, a wasp or a hornet, trapped in the van, biding its time until sun up. Silhouetted against the moonlight it ambled slowly toward the spider, unaware of the pending danger. The spider stands rigid, motionless, and then bang! They lock horns and disappear in a flurry of buzzing wings and flaying legs onto the floor.

Their battle continues for a minute or so, then silence. Who is the victor? I cannot see, but whoever it was, he'll soon be on the prowl again.

I cover my head and sink deep into my sleeping bag.

Apart from visitors from the insect world, other forms of wildlife have been known to visit the works van. As well as cats and dogs, the odd bird (feathered, that is) has unwittingly strayed in through an open window looking for food. The pickings were so good in one van that one small creature couldn't believe his luck, and took up permanent residence there.

It had to be seen to be believed. There had been an issue with timesheets – or the lack of them. When I asked for them, I thought I was hearing things.

'Roddy's eaten them,' came the reply.

'And who the hell is Roddy?' I asked, a little baffled. As far as I knew, we didn't have any Roddys on the firm, and if we did, I'd have surely heard about his funny eating habits.

'He's Roddy the Rodent, a mouse,' said Tony, 'and he lives with us. He used the timesheets to build his house.'

'I've heard some daft excuses in my time,' I said, 'but this takes the biscuit.'

'It's true,' said Albert, and just to prove it, he showed me Roddy's little house.

If I hadn't seen it with my own eyes, I wouldn't have believed it. There hidden under the passenger seat was a red Nescafé mug. Inside was a little nest, neatly furnished with chewed-up timesheets.

'And where is he now then?' I asked out of curiosity.

'He's gone out,' said Tony.

'Gone out!' This was getting dafter by the minute.

'It's true,' said Albert again. 'If we leave the door open he nips out for a look around.'

'We thought we'd lost him once,' said Tony. 'We were worried stiff, the thought of him lost in a garden full of cats and other nasty animals, not to mention the tawny owls who may be looking for a quick snack.'

'Poor thing,' I said. 'Did he come back?'

What was I saying? What was I thinking? Even I was beginning to feel concerned for Roddy the little rodent adventurer, lost in the wilds of Derbyshire.

Life was good; the future looked bright and I enjoyed my new-found role in the firm. We had some wonderful gardens to look after, and lovely people to deal with, but there was a thorn in my side; Darren.

Darren, a long-haired hippy type character, had been Cyril's right hand man for some time. He declined the offer of promotion, stating his reason to be that he didn't want the responsibility. This was a decision he obviously came to regret, and as time went on, his resentment towards me became more and more evident.

A battle of personalities began to develop between the two of us.

He spoke in a sarcastic manner, doing all he could to make life difficult, trying to goad me into retaliation. If that didn't work, he'd switch his attention to Albert, who was easy going. But Albert had one big advantage; he was hard of hearing. Darren's mickey-taking and insulting remarks often drew nothing more than a smile from Albert, which infuriated him all the more in his quest for a quick laugh.

I made a great effort to win him over, but Darren seemed to have a Jekyll and Hyde personality. One day he could be friendly and outgoing, couldn't do enough for you; the next, he seemed to be consumed in dark moods, nasty and irritable, looking for trouble. Determined not to let him get the better of me, I bided my time, and waited until he moved on to pastures new. Eventually,

Darren decided it was time to go, but not before we had the satisfaction of seeing him brought down a peg or two, and from an unlikely source.

He hoped to embarrass us all one more time before he left, by opening his big mouth. But this time Darren was to meet his match.

We were working on the garden of Mr and Mrs Grace. They lived in a leafy suburb of Derby. Both were doctors, close to retirement, and they had been on our books for some years. The house was being made ready to be sold so they could move to a new bungalow up in Derbyshire. Mr Grace was a fine Scottish gentleman, who never seemed to be without his beloved pipe. He always seemed to have a serious, studious look on his face, which belied his humorous character. Both were keen gardeners, and wanted everything left in tip-top condition for the new owners.

The peace of the day was broken by Darren, who from the top of a cherry tree began to chant, 'UNITED, UNITED, UNITED.'

His yobbish cries were directed at a man and a boy walking down the street; it was none other than Brian Clough, or 'Cloughie', as he was affectionately known. The famous manager of Derby County was out walking with one of his sons.

The embarrassing tirade continued. They crossed the road, and made their way over to the tree, where they both stood looking up at Darren.

Cloughie's face was deadly serious. The little chap looked up at his dad, waiting, as if he already knew what was about to happen.

Cloughie never said a word, just stared directly into Darren's eyes. It had the desired effect, for the tone of Darren's voice began to change. It became lower, softer, before finally disintegrating into a feeble squeak, then silence. The realisation of who was standing before him had suddenly hit home.

The commotion brought out the doctors and one or two

neighbours, who arrived just in time to hear Cloughie's response. Speaking in those familiar nasal tones, loud enough for the whole street to hear, he said; 'I thought it a little strange to hear monkeys in the gardens of England, but now I can see you're not a monkey, you're a girl ... no, wait a minute, you're not a girl either, so what am I looking at?'

'Darren,' came the timid answer.

'But that's a boy's name, and if you are a boy, I feel sorry for you.'

We all stood there with big grins on our faces. Even deaf Albert could hear what was going on.

Darren had dared to ridicule the Derby boss, a man famous for plain speaking. He had come unstuck, and his little potshot had been answered by a full broadside from Cloughie.

We had a brief conversation about the state of the Derby pitch and he was on his way, but not before another parting shot at Darren.

'By the way Darren, which United do you support?'

'*Leeds* United.'

'Oh no, now I really do feel sorry for you, young man.'

No words can describe the feeling of expectation around this old football town when Brian Clough and his sidekick Peter Taylor had breezed into Derby in 1967. Too long in the wilderness, this old footballing club had been given a kick up the backside and raised from its slumber. The place was buzzing; there was a pride about the town. Even people with no previous interest in the game were talking football. The old days had returned and we were heading back to where we belonged, in the top flight. Nothing seemed impossible. They delivered the second division championship as promised, and then the league title. If Clough and Taylor said they'd do it, it was as good as done. There is no doubt the European Cup would have taken pride of place in the Derby County trophy cabinet if it hadn't have been for an unfortunate turn of events, a few years later.

On 15 October 1973 we were in the Clough neighbourhood

again, working close to his house on Ferrers Way. There seemed to be a commotion. It was Clough and Taylor, both seemed angry, annoyed, gesturing and pointing to a pack of reporters outside on the street. They had just resigned. Clough and Taylor were on their way to pastures new, and with them went the hopes and dreams of the people of Derby.

A few years later, I was sad to learn of Darren's death. We didn't know it at the time, but he was heavily into drugs. He was only a young man when he died from an overdose. Looking back, this must have been one of the reasons for his mood swings and irrational behaviour. It was a tragic waste of a life: he was intelligent, and could have gone far in anything, had he put his mind to it.

The boss always said; 'The ladies are the gardeners of this country, and most of the time you will be dealing with them, so beware! They know what they are talking about, and so must you.'

He couldn't have said a truer word. As I have found over the years, more often than not it's the lady of the house who seems to take charge. They all seem to be experts, the gentlemen happy to leave them to it, content in growing the odd vegetable or two.

A typical example was Mrs Player. She lived at Ednaston Manor in Derbyshire. Now, she really knew what she was talking about when it came to the subject of gardening. Coming from a family of gardeners, Mrs Player had created one of the most interesting gardens to be found anywhere in the land. She was overseeing a new planting scheme she had designed for Lady Scarsdale at Kedleston Hall. We had the job of preparing and planting the new stock. This gave us the opportunity to go over to the manor to see the house and gardens for ourselves.

Ednaston Manor was built between 1913 and 1919, and designed by the famous architect Sir Edwin Lutyens. The gardens were influenced by Miss Gertrude Jekyll, the famous garden designer of the time. It wouldn't be the last time I'd come across the work of these famous people. Their names would pop up more than once in the future.

The gardens began to develop in 1948 on the arrival of Mrs Player. They are magnificent, and are now recognised as among the best around. Containing many specimen trees and shrubs, there is interest in every turn, with woodland paths and border walks, and a stunning azalea border, a theme she was to recreate at Kedleston where the new border, close to the rose garden, covered an area that led up to the tennis courts. Mrs Player directed the operation, with the help of Lady Scarsdale and a little verbal encouragement from the Commodore.

Commodore Jackson Whayman was a family friend. He often accompanied her Ladyship around the grounds. We found him to be a jovial, friendly character, always willing to stop and talk on almost any subject you cared to mention.

The Commodore had a secret.

For some time, he'd been growing a clematis, a climbing plant, for her Ladyship's new border. When the time came, he'd been looking forward to presenting it to Lady Scarsdale as a surprise. He was as pleased as punch as he took me to a secluded part of the garden to show me his efforts. He would be the first to admit he knew nothing about gardening, and for him, and not being the green-fingered type, to attempt to grow anything was a miracle in itself.

'What do you think of my clematis, George?' he asked, enthusiastically. 'I've been growing it for some time. It's a surprise for Ottilie. She says I am a useless gardener, but this will show her!'

'Well, Commodore, it will certainly be a surprise, and I would be the first to admit, it *is* a prize specimen, but you have a problem. It's a weed.'

'WHAT!' He couldn't believe his ears.

'You've been training a weed against the wall, Commodore. Bindweed, to be precise.'

'Bind what? What the hell is that?' the Commodore asked again, looking a little puzzled.

'As I said, it's a weed.'

'But what about those lovely white flowers?' he said, his eyes pleading with me to be wrong.

'It is beautiful, Commodore, but it's very tenacious, and if it gets into her Ladyship's new border, she'll never get rid of it. I'm sorry, Commodore, there's no doubt about it, it's a weed.'

Embarrassed by his mistake, he ripped the whole lot from the wall, and made me promise never to say a word to her Ladyship, a promise that was faithfully kept, but I couldn't wait to tell Woofy. He seemed to know all about it and seemed a little annoyed at the news.

'You didn't tell him, did you?' he asked, a look of disappointment written all over his face.

During the summer months we worked long hours, with every-one expected to do overtime. We were always on the move; a team of mobile gardeners, travelling all over Derbyshire and beyond.

We were out on the road early. Morning has always been my favourite time of day. To be in a beautiful garden with the morning dew still on the roses is a spiritual experience.

It wasn't all work. A day out at the Chelsea Flower Show was certainly an eye-opener for the young ones amongst us. To see flowers grown to perfection and to 'look and learn', as Mick put it, it was an inspiration to us all.

Meetings were held once a month. More of a social occasion, we would all gather at Mick's house to discuss any problems or concerns anyone might have. The main topic was always the customer, and generally they were nice people to deal with, give or take the odd one or two.

Those early years were a time of learning and discovery. Every day was different, and with an infinite variety of gardens to work in, there was always something new to look forward to and a few surprises on the way.

Arriving at Kedleston Hall one morning, we found the whole place had been taken over by the film industry. The gardens were alive with film stars, directors and film crews; many had already been at work for hours. We were greeted by what was probably some sort of set manager. A slim woman, with short black hair and dark glasses, dressed head to toe in black leather, a typical luvvie type with 'darling this' and 'darling that'. She really fancied herself – and Mick, who seemed her favourite from the start.

'Before you start work, come and have some breakfast,' she said. Then in typical luvvie fashion, she linked arms with us and led us over to the mobile canteens that had been set up in the stabling yard.

We'd already eaten, but we couldn't resist the smell of that freshly-cooked food and helped ourselves to generous plates of bacon and eggs, tea and toast, while she explained the situation. They had come to Kedleston and other locations in Derbyshire to film the new Ken Russell production of *Women in Love*, starring Oliver Reed, Alan Bates and Glenda Jackson.

Filming that day was scheduled to be outside in the garden, and what she said next nearly made us choke on our bacon buttics. 'We are going to need your cooperation,' she said.

Our eyes lit up at the prospect of being involved in the movies, and then immediately dimmed again when she gave us our instructions – all we had to do was keep our mouths shut.

'It's simple,' she said. 'When you hear the word "ACTION", all you have to do is stand still and keep quiet.'

It seemed like Hollywood had come to town, and with the order to stop and stand still ringing out every few minutes, work became impossible, so we gave up, and wandered off to soak up the atmosphere. The place was buzzing. Famous faces sat in quiet corners studying film scripts.

Oliver Reed could be seen strutting up and down in front of the hall, dressed in a jacket of brown and gold stripes, looking skyward, preparing himself for the day ahead.

Film crews prepared props and lighting, dragging cables and equipment from one part of the garden to another, and in amongst them all there was Lady Scarsdale, watching over her beloved garden, ready to give an ear-bashing to anyone with careless feet. It wasn't long before she found a victim.

One unfortunate gentleman decided to take a short cut through her Ladyship's agapanthus bed. She blew her top. She didn't need a megaphone; anyone within a fifty-yard radius stopped dead in their tracks thinking filming was about to start. She then let fly with a torrent of verbals that hit the poor fellow like a shockwave. 'Tell that fool to get his big feet out of my flower bed!' she raged. He never dared look back, as he made a dash for the cover of the churchyard.

Filming that day was taking place under one of the old beech trees, close to the church. The set manager seemed quite friendly towards Mick, and after a little persuasion, she managed to sneak us quite close to the action. The scene involved Jennie Linden, Eleanor Bron and Alan Bates, who demonstrated the art of eating a fig. We watched as he did take after take, eating fig after fig, until the director was satisfied. We had an interesting conversation with the soundman; his recording equipment had been set up next to the steps, close to the old aviary. He had worked on many big productions, including *The Sound of Music*. We couldn't get over just how short some of the shots at the dinner party scene had been. He told us 'You're lucky if you do more than a couple minutes, I once did seven minutes on *The Sound of Music*, but that was exceptional.'

Women in Love was released in 1969. A romantic drama set in 1920s industrialised Britain, it was a beautifully made film and we had been lucky enough to see some of it being made. It was wonderful to see the final outcome of the scenes we watched being filmed once they were edited into one continuous sequence.

The movie makers moved on, but it wouldn't be the last time we would get to see them in action. In the years to come there were numerous other movies, television programmes and adverts made at Kedleston.

Part of the TV series *Nanny* was filmed at the hall. Set in the 1930s, it starred Wendy Craig. The old stables and yard were to be given a makeover, ready for filming. The stables were in a state of disrepair. They must have been an impressive sight in the past, providing stabling for over twenty horses. Part of the main stables had to be cleared. This building in itself was a work of art, with its vaulted ceilings and its woodwork. We had the job of clearing out some of the junk that had accumulated over the years, ready for the set builders to do their work.

Just a few of the old stalls were refurbished. Once cleaned, painted and varnished, they looked as good as new. New name plates were made, bearing the names of Byron, Corby, Captain, Thunder and Bess, faithful servants from years gone by. For a brief moment, the old stables were alive again.

A massive water trough complete with hand pumps appeared in the yard. Being three to four feet deep, it looked as though it must have weighed several tons, even empty. Imagine the look on our faces when after filming, two members of the film crew picked it up and marched out of the yard towards the dump to burn it. Such was the skill of those set makers it was hard to tell papier mâché and polystyrene from the real thing.

We all got a little hot under the collar the day glamour came to Kedleston. An advertising company arrived to make a TV advert for a famous ladies' underwear company. To show off their latest range of lingerie, several young models were hired for the filming. This was to take place in and around the rose garden. Little did we realise it at the time, but we had a star in our midst, Woofy, who was persuaded by the director to give us a display of his acting skills.

'You're a natural, Mr Woof,' she assured him. 'There will be little need for make-up, and I just want you to be yourself.'

So with a little dab of a powder puff, hoe in hand, Woofy went forth. Surrounded by a bevy of beauties with almost nothing on, he made his way down to the rose garden, ready for his big part.

His role was to play himself, a gardener merrily hoeing away amongst the roses. Suddenly he catches sight of some scantily clad ladies mysteriously appearing from out of the rhododendron bushes.

The cue for his big scene. All he had to do was to look up in amazement, take his hat off and scratch his head. With no script to learn, the cameras were ready to roll.

Take one; the ladies came out of the bushes and ran across the lawn towards Woofy, who played his part perfectly. Unfortunately, he looked straight at the camera.

Take two; one of the ladies caught her negligee on a bush, slipped, and fell ass over teakettle on to the gravel path grazing her knee.

Take three; Woofy dropped his hoe.

We don't know if it was stage fright, or the sight of those ladies with next to nothing on running towards him, but on take four, he dropped his hat.

After one or two more cock-ups, they got it right, and Woofy became a star, if only for a brief period. He was even awarded a small fee for his efforts. The advert was screened nationwide and his small-screen debut was seen by friends and family all over the country. Many called or wrote letters to ask him what it was like to be a star.

I sensed the boss was happy; we worked well together, and seemed to have a lot in common. With the business still in its infancy, Mick was fast building a good reputation. He had moved his family from Nottinghamshire in the early 1960s to set up a small garden service in Derbyshire.

He'd spent all his life in horticulture, working in almost every field of the industry, from market gardening and landscape to rose-growing and private service.

Over the coming years he was to teach me all I know, and I would come to have a deep respect for him, not only as a work colleague, but also as a man. As he predicted, working outdoors was now in my blood and little did I realise just how much there was to learn. The plant world is such a diverse and sometimes bewildering subject, with literally hundreds of thousands of different species of flowering plants throughout the world, all grouped into hundreds of different families. I soon realised I had a lifetime of learning ahead of me. Life outdoors exceeded all my expectations. I was now part of a team, and to me it was the best job in the world.

5

Kidnap, Robbery and Murder

It was Christmas; Kath and I had been out shopping for presents. One of these was a new bicycle for our son Paul. Carrying it through town, we were approached by two plain-clothes detectives.

'Excuse me sir, could we have a word? We are from the Derby CID.' 'They obviously think we've stolen it!' said Kath, rummaging in her bag looking for the receipt.

'It's OK. You're not under arrest,' they assured us. 'We're just looking for volunteers. We would like you to take part in an identity parade. If you could spare us an hour of your time we would be very grateful, and there'll be a small fee for your trouble.' Kath laughed her socks off; 'I always said you looked like a crook!'

I was intrigued at the prospect, and with time on my hands I agreed. After all, this would be an experience you don't get every day, and a good tale to tell the family over Christmas dinner. So, like a gentleman, I left Kath struggling with two bags and a bike while I made my way down to Full Street, Derby's main police station, to take part in a bizarre little episode that would be worthy of a few lines in any crime writer's novel.

After being signed in, a giant of a sergeant led me upstairs to a room where a number of other men were waiting. They were all shapes and sizes. The tall, the short, the young and the old. Dark haired, blond haired and grey. The pretty, the handsome and the pretty well ugly; a real assortment.

With too many volunteers, a few men were selected, given a thank you and paid off with a couple of pounds for their trouble.

The rest of us gathered around the sergeant for a briefing on what was about to happen. The accused will come out first. He will be asked to look at the line-up. If there is anyone he doesn't like the look of, he has the right to dismiss them. He then has the choice of where to stand in the line. If, by any chance, any of you know each other, the accused or the witness, you must speak up and leave the room immediately. We all shuffled into line. A scruffy-looking man came out; I guess he was in his thirties. He had collar-length dark hair and I didn't know him from Adam. After walking up and down the line a couple of times, he decided to plonk himself next to two people who looked of a similar size and build. Myself and a greasy-haired rocker in a leather jacket. Before the witness came out, the sergeant gave us some comforting words. 'Don't worry if you're picked out,' he said, 'you won't be going to jail!'

The witness was a tall, dark-haired woman, immaculately dressed, and very sophisticated. Her face looked familiar; I was sure I knew her from somewhere, but from where I couldn't say. The sergeant read out a statement, outlining the nature of the charges. The man standing next to me had tried to sell the witness a valuable oil painting he'd stolen.

That's when it clicked. I knew her from Wards, the fine art shop in Derby. It was a shop I used to visit. I used to do a bit of painting in what I call my creative period. Whenever I had the chance I'd call in to have a look around, trying to gain inspiration from some of the masterpieces on display there. It didn't work. It just made me realise that mine was a hopeless case, and more often than not, my latest work would end up in the bin with the rest of the rubbish. But the shop was worth a visit just to gaze in admiration at the fine works of art on display. They were all out of my price range, but one day in the future, I hoped I might be able to afford one.

I decided not to mention the witness; after all, I didn't know her, and what possible connection could there be between the crook, the painting, the witness and me? When she approached the line ready for the identification she gave me a glance. I could tell she was thinking the same as me; 'I've seen that ugly mug somewhere before!' but like me she couldn't think where. What the sergeant read out next nearly made me fall over backwards. The painting had been stolen from a private nursing home and I knew all about it, because at the time of the robbery we had been working on the gardens, and had been questioned by the police. What a coincidence! Here I am now, taking part in an identity parade with the man who carried out the robbery. Having robbed a place where I had been working, he was now standing next to me, and to cap it all, he'd taken his ill-gotten gains to Wards, a place I knew well.

She was asked to walk along the line and have a good look at each individual, and if she recognised the thief, indicate to the sergeant by touching his shoulder. Slow and deliberate, she made sure she had a good look at each one of us. She recognised him immediately – or did she? Perhaps she was looking at me. Strange things do happen, and nothing was stranger than this.

Then she stopped directly in front of us for the second time, taking a long last look at the accused, and another somewhat puzzling look at me. To my relief, she placed her hand on his shoulder next to mine. A thought did cross my mind; I know the sergeant said not to worry if you're picked out, but it did make me wonder if this had happened a couple of hundred years ago and she had been a doddery old witness with poor eyesight, I may have found myself on a convict ship with a one-way ticket to Van Diemen's Land.

After the robbery, the hapless crook had taken his swag to the one place on the planet he should have avoided; Wards, the long-established fine art shop. As well as being fine art dealers, they were also valuers, restorers and advisers to many of the great houses in the county, such as Kedleston Hall, where I'd seen them on occasion. Their experts knew every notable work of art for miles around. The lady from Wards recognised the painting immediately, and on the pretence of valuing it, kept the man waiting with a cup of coffee while she went into the back room to telephone the police, leaving the unsuspecting twit sitting there, patiently waiting for them to arrive and arrest him.

As we worked on the gardens of some of the finest houses around, it seemed almost inevitable that some of them would be targeted by thieves. We'd been working on the gardens of a large country mansion at the bottom of Ashbourne Hill. It had been robbed in the night. At the time, it was the biggest art robbery in the Midlands and made headline news. It seemed a mystery to us how the thieves managed to get near the place. A nasty dog stood guard over the house. As soon as you entered the bottom gate, the thing seemed to sniff you out and would start wailing and howling for all it was worth. It was lucky the house was still standing after Dozy Dick nearly set fire to it, and almost blew himself up in the process. In a stupid and reckless attempt to get rid of some autumn leaves, he'd spent hours raking up a massive pile of them. Dick thought it would be a good idea to make a bonfire. The leaves were bone dry, and all it needed was a match. Dick had different ideas; he decided to pour on the entire contents of a petrol can. BOOM! We all thought the Nestlé's factory had gone up as we came running from the back of the house to see Dick jumping around like a Jack-in-a-box with his hair and trousers on fire. He was lucky, suffering no more than a pair of singed eyebrows, an instant haircut and a suntan. Apart from a few burning embers, some of which nearly set fire to some wood close to the house, the pile had been scattered to the four winds, dispersed neatly around the garden waiting for Dick to rake them all up again.

I arrived home from work to find two detectives sitting on my doorstep. 'I've been expecting you,' I said. 'Oh? Why? Do you have any old oil paintings in the attic going cheap?' said the older of the two with a smile on his face. The younger man's face was deadpan, expressionless. He was obviously new at the job, keen and serious; to him everyone looked like a crook. They asked the usual questions. Did you see anything suspicious? Can you trust your mates? 'Did you see any odd-looking people about?' asked the young one. 'Nope, only Dozy Dick,' I said, 'and he's as odd as they come.' 'Why is he odd? Could he have done it?' The daft sod thought he was on the verge of a confession, so I played him along. 'I take it there is a reward, then?' His eyes lit up in excitement; he really believed me. The older man smiled and thanked me for my cooperation, and then said 'Come on, Clouseau!' to his mate as they went on their way. It wouldn't be the last time the law would call, and sometimes it seemed as if burglars were following us around. Thieves broke into the Indian museum at Kedleston Hall and stole part of Lord Curzon's collection, he was the Viceroy of India from 1899 to 1905 (it must have been a midget who carried out the robbery, cutting out a small door panel to gain entrance). They made off with several priceless and irreplaceable items. Some were later found hidden near a badger set, up the Long Walk.

As far as I know, we never had any bank robbers or villains on the firm, but with several teams now in operation, finding the right people for the job could sometimes be difficult. We seemed to get all manner of odds and sods. With a core of skilled men, the rest were made up of characters from all walks of life. Some were good at the job, and some were bad. We had our fair share of loafers, shirkers, layabouts and skivers, with a few scallywags thrown in for good measure.

Then there were the fine weather gardeners. Those who had given up a career in the factory or office for a new life outdoors. Having made the break in the spring or early summer, they had found their perfect job, until the weather changed. Then, with the onset of winter, they were never to be seen again. We had the clever, and the not so clever. But don't let the word 'clever' fool you. We've had more than one representative from the idiot department over the years; people with brains, who have been blessed with more than their fair share of intelligence, but totally lacking in the one vital ingredient – common sense.

We once had a very clever idiot; he's to be called Einstein for legal reasons. He came to help us out in the summer months, having already secured his place at university. He thought a bit of gardening during the summer would be an ideal way to earn some extra cash. From the beginning there was something wrong, something lacking, and I couldn't put my finger on it. He was pleasant enough, well spoken and came from a good family. What he was studying at university I don't know, but it certainly wasn't gumption. To him, it was as rare as hen's teeth. One of his first jobs was to hold a bag while I filled it with brick rubble. After about three shovels had gone in I stopped to ask; 'Einstein, why is there a load of brick ends around your feet?' There was no bottom in the bag. There is no doubt he would have been buried up to his knees if I hadn't have stopped, but that was nothing, compared to his next glorious demonstration of sheer stupidity. Please believe me when I say this event actually happened, and isn't a figment of my imagination.

Spraying some fruit trees, I sent him up to the house to fill a watering can. The sprayer was the old-fashioned pump-action type, almost like a bicycle pump. Back comes Einstein with the water. All he had to do was put the end of the sprayer into the can, and follow me around. I pumped away but nothing happened. 'Have you got the end in, Einstein?' 'Yes,' he said. Again, I pumped away for all I was worth, and again nothing happened. 'Are you sure it's in, Einstein?' 'Yes it's at the bottom of the can,' he assured me. I pumped away furiously, thinking it may be an air lock. This went on for a minute or so, and again nothing happened; by then I'd had enough. 'It must have a blockage Einstein, give me the can and go and fetch a bucket of clean water so we can flush it out. When I took the can I couldn't believe my eyes; it was empty. The can was sound, and with no sign of a leak. I was baffled.

'Einstein, I did send you up to the house for some water, didn't I?' 'Yes,' he said. 'Well, what happened?' 'There was no one in.' He was right, there wasn't anybody in – upstairs in his brain that is. In his case, the little numbskulls who lived in there had walked out years ago and forgotten to close the door. Give me the village idiot any day!

Due to the increasing workload, and under pressure to get the job done, the firm had taken on a Scotsman named Jim who turned out to be a disaster. He had talked his way into the job claiming to be experienced, but it soon became apparent that he didn't have a clue about gardening.

Jim joined the team that was run by my old school pal, Eddie, and it wasn't long before the complaints came flooding in. When asked by one lady to earth up the potatoes with a hoe, a practice of drawing soil up around the growing plants to stop the tubers tuning green, Jim hoed the whole lot out of the ground, leaving them to die in the hot sun. When challenged by the irate customer, Jim replied; 'I can't understand what you are moaning about missus, you told me to hoe the potatoes up, so that's what I've done – hoed them up!' Worse was to come at Mrs Wrights over at Ednaston, were he spayed her beautiful rose garden with weed killer instead of greenfly killer. A very costly mistake; he had to go.

Despite all that had happened, Eddie begged Mick to keep him on, and against his better judgement, he agreed as long as he stuck to the mowing, which he seemed to be good at. It was a decision he would come to regret, for as well as being a useless gardener, Jim was also a loudmouth and a bully, and unfortunately Eddie didn't seem to recognise it.

The third member of Eddie's team was Sid, his brother-in-law. I knew him well. He had worked for years as a gardener at Breadsall Priory, once the home of the famous Erasmus Darwin. It was now owned by the Haslam family, who made their fortune from engineering. When the estate changed hands, for one reason or another, Sid found himself out of a job. He had led a sheltered life on the estate, and being a loner who lived with his parents, he found it difficult to find another.

Working with his brother-in-law Eddie should have been the ideal position for Sid. Always polite and friendly, he would do anything to please his new work mates, a quality easily taken advantage of by the unscrupulous, and it didn't take long for Jim to get his teeth into Sid. What started off as a little teasing soon led to ridicule and humiliation. Eddie, for some reason, was unable to read the situation, or just preferred to ignore it, laughing it off as just a joke and a bit of fun. Jim had the perfect victim in Sid, who took all the abuse and insults thrown at him. He was determined not to give in, to hang on to his new job at all costs.

The office had received a call about a kidnapping from the Derby police headquarters. A lady witnessed two men pulling up alongside a man walking past her house. She watched as they jumped out, wrestled him to the ground, and then dragged him kicking and screaming into the van. 'I bet it's Eddie again,' Mick said to his wife May, and he was right. Eddie could get a little excited sometimes, and easily jump to conclusions. He had been caught up in an incident some weeks earlier, which also involved the police. On a week's holiday, he was shopping in the town centre. Suddenly he caught sight of the works van sitting in a queue of traffic. Eddie didn't recognise the driver. Thinking it had been stolen, he leapt into action and tried to drag the terrified man from his seat, whilst shouting for help from passers-by. After the police were called, the poor fellow explained he was a temporary driver, covering for Eddie himself. After bringing the city centre to a standstill, he was allowed to go on his way.

This time, the situation was more serious. After months of constant abuse from Jim, Sid finally snapped. They had been working on Mrs Thompson's garden at Burley Hill, on the outskirts of Derby. This garden had to be seen to be believed; it must have been the cleanest, tidiest garden in England – perhaps even on the planet. The place was immaculate; why she hired our services, I'll never know. In a two-hour visit, we'd cut the lawns that had already been cut, then have a cup of tea, try to find any whiskers that may have escaped her attention on the front hedge, and then have another cup of tea, have a search around the beds and borders trying to find an elusive weed – to my knowledge, no one ever found one. Then, to finish the visit off, we'd have another cup of tea.

Thankfully, she didn't witness Sid's rampage when he went for Jim, spade in hand, intent on damage. As Eddie told me later, the normally placid Sid just went berserk, chasing him all around the garden, screaming and shouting, Jim's slightly built frame would have been no match for Sid, who was as strong as an ox. It was only being fleet of foot that saved him from a good hiding or worse. Sid couldn't be calmed; he took off down the road heading for home.

Eddie panicked – the penny had finally dropped. He now realised how serious the situation was, but it was the thought of Sid's father, Tom, on the warpath that worried him the most. I'd worked with Tom; he was an old farmer, strict as they come, not a man to be crossed. If Sid got to him first, the consequences wouldn't bear thinking about. They had to find him and quick, try to calm him, and hope he didn't tell his dad.

Sid didn't have a clue where he was when Eddie and Jim finally caught up with him. At first they tried a little gentle persuasion, but he was having none of it, so in desperation, they manhandled him into the back of the van. This made matters worse; all hell broke loose as Sid began screaming, kicking and punching at the doors trying to get out. They stopped to try and calm him down, but he escaped again. He ran off down the road, this time for good. Distraught and lost, Sid was eventually taken home by a passer-by and never returned to his job. Jim was sacked, and as Eddie feared, Tom went on the warpath. Luckily his retribution was only verbal, but the whole sorry episode caused a rift in the family that was to last for years.

*   *   *

There have been occasions when people have walked off the job. Usually it's someone new, who suddenly finds the hard work isn't for them. Sometimes it's the weather, too hot or too cold. One poor chap walked out of the job at the end of the summer; it was only September when he said he didn't realise how cold the winter would be.

One hot summer's day, two young lads went for a pub lunch and never came back. We'd been working on the garden of a terraced house in the old brewery town of Burton on Trent. I'd warned them not to be too long, as the customer had always been a miserable old so-and-so and would be watching the clock to make sure he had his money's worth. 'We'll be back well within the hour,' Dave assured me. That was the last I saw of them.

Dave and John were both reliable, so it seemed a little unusual when they didn't return on time. The man inside kept coming out to have a look around; he didn't say anything, but I knew he wasn't at all pleased. It was well over the hour when I decided to go and drag them out, thinking perhaps they were in a card game they couldn't get out of, or at the worst, in trouble with the locals.

The man looked a bit of a bruiser, coarse, with a hard-looking face, and a tattoo on the side of his neck. 'Are you the landlord?' I asked. 'Landlady!' came a terse reply. Oops! 'I'm looking for two young lads; they came here for lunch about an hour ago.' 'And who the hell are you?' asked another ugly-looking gorilla sitting in the corner. I felt I'd just walked into that bar in *Star Wars*. Something had gone off; I could sense it, there was an atmosphere. Whatever that pub was called, I don't recall, but an apt description would be 'The Bucket of Blood'. 'They're with me, we're working just up the road. They should have been back some time ago.' 'Well, they won't be coming back for a long time – they've been arrested.' She seemed quite smug with herself. 'Arrested for what?' I asked in disbelief. 'Attempted robbery. They tried to break in last night, intent on robbing the place. I disturbed them, so they fled empty handed. I recognised them as soon as they walked into the bar, so I called the police.' 'So let's get this straight – they tried to rob you last night and thought "that seems a nice pub, let's go back tomorrow for a pie and a pint." It's too daft to laugh at!' 'I don't like your tone,' she said, 'you had better go!' She didn't have to ask twice. With the rest of the inmates of that fine hostelry now beginning to stir, I got out while the going was good. Talk about a drama queen. She supposedly saw them from the bedroom window in the half-light of the morning. It was probably someone creeping around the yard looking for some metal beer barrels to steal.

Dave said it was exciting at first. They watched as several police cars turned up. They thought it was a drugs bust or something until the cops rushed in and wrestled them to the ground. They protested their innocence, told them where they were working, and begged them to go up to the house to see me, but instead they were carted off to the Burton nick and that's where they had been for the last twelve hours.

How many times do we judge people without really knowing anything about them? The miserable old man at the house seemed a different person when I explained to him what had happened to the lads, most sympathetic and concerned. It was then I realised I had never really spoken to him before. I just assumed he was a miserable old sod who didn't want to talk, but I couldn't have been more wrong. When he died a few years later, I was amazed to learn about his past. During the Second World War, he had served as a pilot in the RAF and fought in the Battle of Britain. In fact he was a Spitfire pilot, an ace and a hero, and highly decorated, as the tributes in the national and local newspapers confirmed.

Tony had dashed up from the bottom of the garden. He was out of breath and could hardly speak; his face ashen, as white as a ghost. 'Quick, dial 999!' he said, 'there's a body on the compost heap!' 'Seems a funny place to bury a body,' said Albert. 'I know times are hard but there's no need for that, perhaps it's her husband. 'It hasn't been buried Albert, ya daft sod, it's been disposed of!' said Tony. He was adamant someone had been murdered, done in, their body thrown over the fence and hidden in the compost heap. 'We'd better go down and have a look,' I said, but Tony would have none of it, he was terrified. 'I saw part of a leg, and that's enough for me,' he said. 'You go if you will, but I'm going to the house to tell Mrs Griffiths to phone the police.' The house was on the old Burton road. The fine old Victorian building had extensive grounds, but alas, like many of the handsome properties in the area, it has now suffered the fate of being turned into a nursing home.

Albert and I stopped dead in our tracks; our blood ran cold. Tony was right. There was a body lying there, as he described, just part of a leg visible. Whoever did it had gone to the trouble of trying to conceal it by covering it with old grass cuttings. The smell was awful. It could have lain there for years, undetected, apart from by the flies and the maggots, erupting like little volcanoes from the rotting corpse. 'I knew it,' said Albert. 'I bet it's her husband. She's done him in and dumped him on the compost heap!' As grisly as it was, we had to make sure. Albert, who didn't seem to have a sense of smell, picked up a stick and began to uncover more of the leg. 'I can tell you one thing,' he said, 'whoever it is comes from New Zealand.' 'How you can tell, Albert?' I asked. 'He has a tattoo.' I moved in for a closer inspection. 'That's not a tattoo Albert, it's a stamp, a New Zealand lamb stamp!'

What we thought was a body was in fact the contents of the family freezer, thrown out after one of the power cuts of the early 1970s. The sides of beef, pork and frozen chickens had formed a human shape with a leg of lamb in the perfect position to scare the living daylights out of Tony, as he poked around in curiosity to uncover what he thought was a human leg. It fooled us all, and it's a good job there weren't any mobile phones about then. We'd have called the police, and looked a right bunch of idiots in the process. But there was a murder some years ago, and it was someone close to our hearts.

We had known the 'gentleman' for many years. He was a good friend and a neighbour, and we'd once landscaped his garden. He came from a place called Indian Queens in Cornwall. He supposedly had relatives all over the world. He seemed to be a bit of a loner, having moved up to Derbyshire many years previously to get away from it all. He did come to the odd party or two, but apart from that, he kept himself to himself. His only pleasure seemed to be a drink and a smoke, and as far as I can remember, I never heard him say a bad word against anyone.

A few days had passed before the robbery came to light. No one had seen or heard anything of him. It was thought the old man had taken himself off to Cornwall to visit friends or relatives, and coming from a family of travellers, it wouldn't be unusual to suddenly get a postcard from the other side of the world, but it soon came apparent he was missing, and after a long and fruitless search, we thought he'd been abducted, but he wasn't a rich man, and with no contact or ransom note, his whereabouts remained a mystery.

The news of his death came as a big shock to us all, but it was the way he died, murdered in the most hideous and sinister way, which was hard to bear. When something like this happens close to home, it makes you realise just how fate can deal a cruel hand, and how tragedy can strike at any time. The robbers came at night. There had already been several attempted break-ins in the neighbourhood, so people were on the alert, but it was the level of violence they used just to steal what amounted to a few almost worthless ornaments that angered us the most.

We didn't mind so much about the garden ornaments, they were worthless cast statues, and the mindless idiots must have busted a gut trying to lift them over the fence, but the loss of the old gentleman, with his smiling face, who had always been there, summer and winter, sitting in his favourite spot by the pond, beer tankard and pipe in hand, was hard to bear. It was

Kath, my wife, who found him, or what was left of him. Out in the garden one day, she had the feeling she was being watched. It was then she made the grim discovery; the old gentleman looking down on her from the oak tree in our garden. Having witnessed the robbery, they silenced him by chopping his head off and hanging it on the tree, disposing of the body in spite, so we couldn't glue him together again.

6

All That Glitters

The cannonball was found not far from the old Derby road, on the south side of the town. It must been there for over 200 years, so the experts at the Derby museum told us. It was probably left there by Bonny Prince Charlie's invading army as he passed through Ashbourne, they concluded. Many objects have been found over the years, and more often than not, just like the old cannonball, they were to be found lying on the surface. Most of it was junk: old brass buttons, keys and a few worthless coins. Then occasionally the odd bit of silver and gold, long thought lost and forgotten, would suddenly reappear. Many are the times we've returned some long-lost keepsake to a grateful owner. Some of them have been worthless, but of great sentimental value.

Not all people have been grateful. Mick, my old boss, once found a wallet containing thousands of pounds lying in a shrubbery. When he took his find to the house, he was astonished to hear its owner say 'I wondered were that had got to!' receiving no thanks at all for his honesty. A medieval coin was found which had been lying around in a garden for hundreds of years, just waiting for us to come along and pick it up. It was the same with a pearl and gold ring, found in the garden of a derelict cottage up in the Peak District.

Our fortunes really began to change the day I was given an old metal detector by an uncle of mine. Now we began digging stuff up all over the place; nails, buttons and bits of old wire and junk, junk and more junk. With the help of the wonderful detector, we found nothing but junk.

The church sits on a hill, but the village sits in a sleepy hollow. With the Sutton Brook winding through its meadows, Sutton-on-the-Hill is off the beaten track, and is one of the quietest of places. Sutton Hall is a fine Gothic-style building dating back to 1819. Formally a vicarage, it sits overlooking woodland where masses of golden daffodils are to be found in the spring.

The hall is the home of the Buckston family, who have lived there for generations. Well known in the cricket world, the family have produced some prominent players who have taken the field for Derbyshire, such as George Buckston in the 1920s and his son Robin, who was captain of Derbyshire during the 1960s. Quiet and softly spoken, with the typical style and dress of the landed gentry, Mrs Buckston was a charming woman who always made us feel at home, especially in the tea and cakes department. There was always an enjoyable atmosphere as we all gathered around the huge kitchen table with the rest of the house staff for the morning break. There, the cook would serve up generous helpings of tea and toast.

The gardens were a pleasant mixture of lawns and shrubberies. We made good use of the kitchen garden, growing fruit and vegetables for the house. There were some old greenhouses, used for growing tomatoes, cucumbers, and the odd nectarine or two. One of the main features of the garden was an old yew hedge with no form or shape. It was a monster of a hedge. To see its silhouette in the half-light of day, it wasn't hard to imagine a herd of elephants at the end of the garden.

A storm had brought down a section of old garden wall. It was the job of Fred and I to set about clearing the dense undergrowth, ready for the insurance assessors to do their work. It opened up a piece of ground that hadn't been disturbed for years, so Fred suggested we give the detector a try. Up came the usual stuff, mostly old wall nails and bits of copper wire, all found in the top few inches of the soil. One signal, however, had us digging beyond the usual depths. The excitement began to build as I dug deeper and deeper. It was too much for Fred; he took over. He began to go at it like a badger, digging for all he was worth, and what a sight it was! This was workman's bum in all its glory. He must have dug down over a foot, then he hit something; 'It's a box!' he cried. 'A metal box! It looks like a jewellery box, and there seems to be more than one. I think we've hit the jackpot!' cried Fred.

The box measured about eight by six inches. It was hinged, with a clasp on the front that was rusted solid, resisting all our attempts to open it. 'There's definitely something inside,' said Fred, shaking the box as we made our way to the potting shed to open it. The clasp was so rusted it had to be smashed off with a hammer and chisel before the grand opening.

'Now I know what Carter must have felt like, Fred.' 'What's he got to do with it? And who the 'eck's Carter anyway?' 'You know who I mean Fred, Carter and Carnarvon, of King Tutankhamen fame.' 'King who?' 'They discovered his tomb in the Valley of the Kings.' 'Never heard of the place.' 'Well, when they broke into the tomb, they saw wonderful things.' 'Cut the crap and get on with it,' said Fred, impatient to see the riches we had found. 'One last thing, Fred, you do realise this could be some long lost family heirloom, and if it is, we'll have to let the family know.' 'Yes, of course,' he said, with a look of disappointment written all over his face. 'This is it, Fred, are you ready?'

At last the box was open, and there it was, in all its glory. A dead budgie. We'd been digging in a budgie's graveyard. Instead of buried treasure, all we had was a box full of beaks, bones, feathers, and a rusty old bell. 'Well, I hope you're going to tell them about Bertie the Budgie or whoever it was,' said Fred. 'I'm sure they'll want to know, and what about your mate Carter? I hope he had better luck than us.' At that we put him back in his box, and laid him to rest back in the budgie graveyard.

Of all the things to find, it had to be a budgie. At home we never had any luck with budgies. I've buried a few in my time, but this is the first one I've dug up, and had to bury again. I seem to give them the kiss of death whenever I get near to them.

'So you've been to a few budgie funerals then?' asked Fred, as we reflected on our disappointment over a cup of tea. 'Well, for a start, there was Boris. His funeral was the grandest of them all.' Boris's mum, a Miss Alison, lived in the Rose Hill area of Derby. Born in Victorian times, she was one of the tiniest women I've ever seen and would have won any Queen Victoria lookalike competition hands down. The house was like a time capsule, full of furnishings and decor from another age. She would invite us into the parlour for tea. There she would reminisce about times gone by. There had been many changes over her long years. The Rose Hill of her childhood would have been a totally different world than the multicultural society of today.

Her passion was the Arboretum opposite her house. It was England's first public park, donated to the town by the Strutts, a family of wealthy industrialists. Work on the park began in 1839. Designed by John Claudius Loudon, its completion was marked by a parade through the streets of Derby for the grand opening on 16 September 1840. The park covers seven hectares and one of its unusual features is the serpentine pathways and mounds said to have influenced Fredrick Law Olmsted in his designs for Central Park in New York.

The Arboretum suffered decades of neglect, but Miss Alison remembered it from her days as a young woman in Edwardian times, when it was the pride of Derby. It was a place where people would gather on Sundays to listen to the band play, or just to stroll amongst its many flower displays. Not the mad rushing world of today but a slower, gentler way of life. 'People seemed to have more time for each other in them days,' she would say.

She must have been in her nineties when she called us in to help. You could see the garden had been well loved and looked after. It was almost as if it had been transplanted from a quaint cottage somewhere in the country, being well stocked with a variety of cottage style plants. Her favourite, roses, grew in abundance, alongside honeysuckle and clematis, carefully trained against the red brick garden walls.

We called on our usual day, but this time I was without my regular partner, who was on holiday. Instead, I had my old school pal Eddie for company, and I couldn't have chosen a more unsuitable workmate for what was about to happen.

She was always friendly and cheerful, but on this day we were greeted by a tearful Miss Alison. 'Boris is dead!' she said. 'I'd like you to dig a little grave for him over by the roses.' She handed me a piece of paper indicating the size of Boris's grave, which was a bit peculiar to say the least. Her instructions were to dig a hole eighteen inches by eighteen inches, and a foot deep. At the bottom of this, another hole was to be dug, measuring one foot by seven inches, also a foot deep.

'Are you sure Boris is a budgie?' queried Eddie, as we set about digging the grave. 'This hole is big enough for a good-sized parrot, or vulture,' he quipped. Now I'd seen Boris on many occasions, and I assured Eddie that unless she'd been fattening him up over the last two weeks, he was just your average-sized budgie. That was it; we started giggling and couldn't stop. We were the same at school, we'd only have to look at each other and we were off on a laughing fit, often getting a bash around the ears off some irate teacher who thought we were laughing at them. It had happened once before when I worked with Eddie. Dear old Mrs Eaton lived at the top of Ashbourne Hill. She invited us in for a cup of tea. Being a little hard of hearing, she used to stand close, sometimes too close for comfort. On one particular occasion she stood inches from us, staring at our mouths, trying to pick up on our conversation and without sign language it was impossible, all we got was 'Hey, what, come again, eh, sorry, excuse me, hey, what, come again, eh, sorry...' It went on for some time, until we could stand it no longer. We both cracked up and ran screaming from the house in uncontrollable laughter, much to her dismay. For that to happen in front of Miss Alison would be a disaster.

We had to keep our backs to the house; Miss Alison was watching from the window, waiting for our signal to bring out Boris. We had to delay as long as possible to try to compose ourselves, ready for what would be without doubt an emotional occasion. Eddie spotted something in the soil. A small silver-looking object, possibly a good luck charm, it was hard to tell, but the diversion was enough to calm us down, giving us time to prepare to bury Boris. Miss Alison carried Boris in a little shoebox coffin, decorated with a posy of flowers. As we made our way to the prepared plot, I gave her the object we had found. I thought it might cheer her up, but it seemed to have the opposite effect, as if triggering some distant memory. She seemed sadder than ever. I didn't dare look at Eddie, knowing if I made eye contact it would be curtains for the both of us. All was fine until Miss Alison said; 'Would you like to have a last look at Boris before we lay him to rest?' She removed the lid, and there he was, lying on a bed of cotton wool, on his back and with his feet in the air, surrounded by all his toys and possessions, ready for his journey into the budgie afterlife. 'He always likes to look his best,' said Miss Alison, pointing to a mirror. There was also a packet of Trill, the seed that makes budgies bounce with health. He's going to need a good dose of that before he starts to chirp again, I'm thinking. Eddie must have been thinking the same. That was it; this time he really lost it, he couldn't contain himself any longer and had to turn away. Bent double, trying to hide his face, he made a strange noise, something between a squeak, squeal and wheeze, trying to stifle the laughter within. Almost as bad, I had my head in the hole, pretending to remove some last bit of earth, trying to gain a few more precious seconds before we both had to turn and face Miss Alison.

I managed to compose myself just in time, but Eddie stood there a complete wreck, with tears rolling down his face. My prayers weren't for Boris. They were for Eddie, hoping she didn't

catch sight of him, but they went unanswered. Suddenly she grabbed his arm, we steeled ourselves, ready for a good telling off, but to our amazement she said. 'Don't cry, Eddie, there's no need to be sad, Boris is at peace now.'

When we laid Boris to rest, the reason for the oversized grave became apparent. Boris's coffin was placed in the smaller bottom chamber at the bottom of the hole. Then an old paving slab placed on top. This was to stop any 'varmints' from digging him up again, as Miss Alison put it. Now resting in his little tomb, Boris was indeed a pharaoh amongst budgies, unlike some of the hapless birds we kept at home. It wasn't through ignorance or neglect – perhaps living with us gave them their suicidal tendencies, I don't know, but they always seemed to come to an untimely end.

They all seemed to be called Peter for some reason. I suppose it was logical in a way, we seemed to get through that many, that for future reference one name would be easier to remember. One Peter somehow managed to get inside an old piano and fluttered around making eerie music on the strings; he died of exhaustion before we could get him out. The whole family nearly perished along with another budgie one night, as Mother came screaming into the bedrooms to wake us. The house was full of gas. She had accidently knocked on a gas tap whilst cleaning the cooker and went off to bed. Relieved we weren't all dead, she also had the presence of mind not to switch on the lights and blow us all to bits, but alas, downstairs, yet another Peter had bitten the dust.

There must have been at least three Peters who, at the first opportunity, made a dash for freedom, their sixth sense telling them to get away from our house as soon as possible. Perhaps the most bizarre incident happened one afternoon when I arrived home from school to find yet another Peter was in peril. With Mam and Dad at work, and the kids at school, our house was very cold in winter. Mam had arrived home to find Peter lying stiff at the bottom of his cage. 'I think it's just the cold,' she said. Copying one of the neighbours who had tried the same technique with success, she put the oven on a low heat and attempted to revive him. With Peter lying on a grilling pan, she pushed him gently in and out of the oven, looking for signs of life. On the inward stroke, my sister walked in. The look on her face said it all; she thought Peter was for dinner. Our Dennis, who had been watching the drama unfold, sat there with a devilish grin on his face, and then to my sister's horror said; 'Are we having chips with it, Mam?'

Idridgehay is a small village in the valley of the Ecclesbourne, a few miles from the old lead mining town of Wirksworth. South Sitch ('sitch' meaning stream) had been in the Bemrose family since the turn of the twentieth century. It was now the home of Mr and Mrs Clive Bemrose, whose family owned the Bemrose printing works in Derby. The house, an attractive timber-framed building with a thatched roof, dates back to at least 1621.

The day had been memorable for two reasons. One was for Albert demonstrating his diving skills in the duck pond, and the other was for young Tony discovering gold in the water garden. Renovation of the water gardens became a learning curve for us. With little experience of aquatic plants and rock pools, it soon turned into an interesting and rewarding project, made easier with the help of Mrs Bemrose who was very knowledgeable on the subject.

The day had been unbearably hot, as we dozed away our lunch break under the shade of an old apple tree. Suddenly Albert leapt to his feet. 'I've had enough!' he cried. 'I'm going for a dip.' Before we could stop him, Albert was racing across the lawn, heading for the duck pond. 'Not a good idea, Albert!' I shouted, but it was in a vain. My cries fell on deaf ears, literally – he had always been hard of hearing and didn't hear a word I said. 'Watch this, Tony!' I knew what was coming, and waited for the impact. Albert took off at speed, and flew through the air with all the grace of a hippo. Almost reaching the centre of the pond, he landed with a splat in amongst the ducks, which flew for their

lives. He had plunged deep into the thick black mud, hidden just below the surface. Poor old Albert; what had looked like a pool of clear, cool water was in fact a quagmire of silt and rotting vegetation, built up over many years, although the sight of ducks walking on water should have given him a clue.

Albert was a real stick-in-the-mud, flailing about trying to get out. We arrived to help, but stood well clear as he emerged from the pond looking like something from a swamp monster movie. He was caked in thick black mud; the smell was awful. To make matters worse, he was fully clothed. We made our way towards the house, and the nearest hosepipe. With the heat of the day his clothes were beginning to dry, leaving a trail of mud along the garden path. Mrs Bemrose almost died of fright when she caught sight of him coming through the gate. We hosed Albert down, and left him out to dry. Alone.

It was late afternoon when young Tony struck gold. He spotted a shiny object half buried in the soil. He had found a gold watch. The face and mechanism had long since deteriorated, but the gold itself was perfect, and the inscription on the back could be easily read. The watch belonged to Clive Bemrose, presented to him to mark his twenty-five years with the family firm. Tony took his find to the house. Mrs Bemrose said the old man who tended the gardens had been searching for that watch for years. On our next visit, Mr Bemrose came out to thank Tony, and to his surprise gave him back the watch and a few pounds for his honesty. This was typical of the family. South Sitch became one of our favourite gardens. Work continued on the water gardens for a number of years, until the Bemroses moved to a smaller house some miles away. We were delighted when Mrs Bemrose called on our services again to work on her new garden.

Apart from a few dead budgies and one or two worthless objects, our metal detecting days turned out to be fruitless. It was only a cheap one anyway and eventually broke down and was assigned to the bin, although if it had lasted just a little longer, it could have saved us a lot of time and effort in our search for one very valuable piece of jewellery.

'It's in there somewhere,' he said, as we looked upon the biggest pile of horse muck you've ever seen. The man had done well for himself, owning a chain of garages in and around Staffordshire. He could now indulge his passion for horses, which came with the inevitable by-product; muck. It was to be used on his garden, and our job was to move it to the new rose beds and tree plantations around the stabling block. This time there was a little more incentive to get stuck in. The brooch was worth thousands of pounds, he told us, and there was a substantial reward for whoever found it. He took a wad of notes from his wallet. 'There's a hundred pounds here. I shall leave it up at the house with the wife. She's out shopping, but should be back before you go.' As Albert, Tony and I approached the giant pile, the thought of the reward put a spring in our step. In those days, a hundred pounds was nearly three weeks wages. We agreed to split it three ways, no matter who found the brooch.

We examined each forkful, breaking it down as it went into the barrow, eagerly looking for a glint of diamond or gold, repeating the same process on the rose beds and plantations, tipping it out carefully, spreading it neatly amongst the roses, searching, expecting our prize to appear at any time. Tea arrived towards the end of the day. Most of the muck heap had now been moved, but there was still no sign of the elusive brooch.

'We tried, but I think you must have lost it somewhere else,' I suggested to the lady of the house. 'Lost what?' she said. 'Your brooch. We've been searching this muck heap all day for it.' 'Who told you that? I haven't lost any brooch,' she said. 'Your husband. He's left a hundred pounds reward for whoever finds it.' Her face lit up at that. 'He's kidding,' she said. 'That was just a carrot to make you work hard. He likes to make sure he gets his money's worth.'

Needless to say, we were all fuming. 'I know where this muck fork's going,' said Albert. What idiots we'd been, working our socks off, looking for something that didn't exist. Then to add insult to injury, he turned up with a big grin on his face, just as we were finishing. 'I hope there are no hard feelings, lads,' he said. Did he plan to do it or was it the vengeful look on our faces that made him take out his wallet again, and give us all ten pounds each? There's an old saying; 'It's not the hours you put in. It's what you put into the hours.' Well, we'd certainly put a lot of hours in on that day, and a great deal of effort into the hours!

One unusual find was a truffle. This edible fungus can be found growing underground, in amongst the roots of oak, beech and other broad leaf trees of the forest. The eighteenth-century gastronome Brillat-Savarin called them 'the diamonds of the kitchen', or black gold. Highly prized and valuable, this sought-after delicacy can fetch a high price, and the one we found was a decent size. It was found growing on the roots of a young oak tree. The tree was part of a consignment of trees and shrubs that had been shipped over from the continent ready for a landscaping project in the beautiful city of Bath. A new stabling block had been built at the racecourse, and our job was to plant thousands of trees and shrubs to screen the new building.

We held on to our prize for a few days, declining all offers of a sale, deciding to keep it for ourselves, and cook up some suitable dish to see what all the fuss was about. After a little research, Kath was ready. 'I've decided on fresh salmon with a brie salad, sprinkled with shavings of truffle,' she said, 'and a nice bottle of wine!' Knowing Kath's skills in the kitchen, I knew it would be something to look forward to as I settled down in front of the telly in anticipation. With the meal prepared, all that was left was to add the shavings of truffle. 'It seems a little tough,' said Kath as she struggled with the knife. The outer surface was dry, a little crusty, with some roots of oak still visible. 'I hope it hasn't gone off!' she said. 'I'm going to cut it in half and have a look at the inside.' Even with a sharp knife, it took some cutting. The inside was perfect; jet black, a little spongy but firm. It seemed

OK, but I still decided to have a taste – after all it would only spoil the dinner if we didn't like it. 'What do you think?' said Kath, 'shall we use it?' 'In my humble opinion I think it's overrated, what do you think?' 'Tastes a little rubbery to me,' she said. 'Rubbery... that's exactly what I think.' We looked at each other in a puzzled silence. 'Are you thinking what I'm thinking? she said. 'It can't be, can it?' There was only one way to find out; I made my way over to the cooker and held the piece of 'truffle' over a naked flame. It immediately burst into flames, giving off a black acrid smoke. Our prize truffle turned out to be an old rubber ball. It must have been in the ground for years. The oak roots had grown into its surface. It had become part of the tree, and looked liked the perfect truffle.

7

Going it Alone

I awoke in a cold sweat. A thousand questions and doubts raced through my mind. Have I made the right decision? Should I have waited longer? Have I been a fool? Lying there in the sober light of the early hours seems to sharpen the senses; everything seems clear and the stark reality of your actions begins to hit home. But one thing was certain – there was no going back. Although I was surrounded by close friends and family, I suddenly felt completely alone. From now on I was on my own, and my future and the future of my family were in my hands. Anyone who has ever left a secure job to set out into the unknown, to start their own business, will know what I'm talking about. The mind is suddenly focused; focused on survival.

The crash of Rolls Royce, the miners' strike and three-day weeks meant that the early 1970s were difficult times for us all, but the thought of leaving the firm had been on my mind for some time. Mick and his family had been good to us. With decent pay, job security, and a list of loyal customers, many of whom I'd grown to know so well over the years, it was as good as being my own boss, and leaving would be difficult.

Like most couples, Kath and I wanted to buy our own house, but securing a mortgage on my current wages would be difficult. Mick understood my reasons for leaving. 'Every man is his own agent,' he said. I set up my own business for those very reasons; to better myself, and to get onto the property ladder. He told me to go for it, and not to leave it too late. I should have done it years ago, he said. I agreed to work the rest of the summer and part company in the autumn, but it was actually November when I left. My first big mistake, and little did I realise what I was letting myself in for.

A new phase of my life was about to begin. I couldn't tell what lay over the horizon, but I hoped that the coming decades would turn out to be just as interesting and fulfilling as the first. On 4 November 1974, Kath and I decided to throw caution to the wind and have a go at running our own business. So with two weeks wages as capital, a few old tools and a battered old Morris Minor van worth fifty quid, I became self-employed.

Life from now on would be different, and would depend solely on my own efforts. It was my sixth wedding anniversary. We always joked that we got married on 4 November and the fireworks started the next day, but this time the next day would only bring doubts and worries of an uncertain future.

That first winter in business was without doubt the most insecure period of my life. Now I really was working for a crust. With little or no money coming in, these were difficult times. It didn't take me long to realise I'd made a big mistake by delaying my departure. Winter was upon us, and work was thin on the ground. During those long winter months, there were a few sleepless nights as I began to question the wisdom of my actions. Will I get enough work? And how will I pay the bills? Believe me, going it alone is not for the faint-hearted, especially without any capital or savings to fall back on, but I was young, fit and determined to see it through.

Before leaving, I'd managed to secure a few jobs from family and friends. My first landscaping job was at a pub, the Crown Inn at Heanor in Derbyshire. This provided work for a couple of weeks. Somehow we muddled through to the spring, and remarkably even managed to pay our way. I'd promised to help out the old firm if they were stuck for labour and was asked to continue at Kedleston Hall on a subcontract basis, which was a tremendous help in those early months.

The relationship between my old boss and Mr Curzon had always been a little strained. Mr Curzon was the estate manager, and the next lord in waiting. There had been a disagreement in the past over some garden alterations the firm had carried out at Western Lodge, the home of the Curzons. They never seemed to get on after that, and Mick felt it was only a matter of time before his services at the hall were no longer required.

As predicted, Kedleston Hall and my old firm parted company. I was approached by Lady Scarsdale, who offered me a full-time job at the hall. I was grateful, but declined. I explained that I'd decided to go my own way, and regardless of the outcome, I had to see it through. 'Could you at least do us a couple of days a week?' she asked, so I agreed. This was ideal; it secured wages for two days, leaving me the rest of the week to concentrate on the more profitable landscape work.

Our first enquiry into the mortgage market was a waste of time. Little did I realise that being self-employed, at least three years trading accounts would be required before the bank would even consider a mortgage. That and the lack of a deposit ruled out any hope of us joining the property market for a year or two yet.

Throughout 1975, orders began to come in, and before too long I was working long hours. With a string of regular customers and a good income, I could look forward to the future with confidence for the first time. July saw us partying at the hall. Usually an annual event, these occasions gave the employees and the tenant farmers a chance to get together and to wish the lord and lady well. Held in the main hall, they were always well attended with plenty of food and drink laid on by the hosts, Lord and Lady Scarsdale.

This time, the party was a little special. It was to celebrate Viscount Scarsdale's fiftieth year as Lord of Kedleston. With his Lordship insisting on greeting every guest in person, there was quite a queue when we arrived at 6.30pm. It was a perfect summer evening. Most of the time could be spent outside. The gardens looked beautiful, and Woofy beamed with pride at all the favourable comments.

His Lordship's time was in great demand, with a constant stream of people waiting in line to have a few words, and to congratulate him on reaching this milestone. There were some families, such as the Morleys, Huchingsons and Yates, who had worked the land at Kedleston for generations. Many would have known him as a young man, when he first came to the estate fifty years before. Having lived, worked and grown old together, the respect and affection they had for each other was clearly visible. To mark the occasion, his Lordship was presented with a stone fountain, given to him by the estate. Lady Scarsdale gave an emotional speech in tribute to her husband; both were visibly moved. This was followed by rapturous applause, bringing to an end what had been a memorable evening.

Although the summer of 1975 had been good, 1976 turned out to be the year of the great drought, one of the hottest anyone could remember – before or since. At the beginning of June, it snowed during a cricket match in Derbyshire, and that was it. For the next three months little rain fell, gardens and landscape began to dry up. By midsummer, lawns and fields were brown and parched, flowerbeds struggled to survive, even some mature trees wilted and died. The prolonged dry spell also affected the job and work began to dry up. Some landscape works were put on hold. With the ground like concrete and turf unavailable, I had to rely solely on the maintenance work built up over the last two years. One or two of them laid me off, saying there's no point in cutting the grass when there's nothing to cut.

As the summer wore on, the landscape began to resemble that of a foreign land. The lush green fields were now a patchwork of brown and harvest gold, and even the pubs couldn't keep up with the demand for beer. Water had to be used sparingly, although that didn't bother old Fred. 'I never touch the stuff!' he said. Ever since the doctor told him a pint of Guinness was good for his health, he'd drunk nothing else. What he thought they made

Guinness with, we can only guess. The dry weather did have its compensations; we did manage to get away for a week's holiday, our first since we were married, and the little work we had was easy going, not the battle of being up to your neck in weeds and wet grass normally endured during a typical English summer.

At Kedleston, some major rewiring works were in progress. With little to do in the gardens, we were drafted in to help out, giving us a chance to see some parts of the hall that were normally out of bounds. The old wine cellars under the west wing had to be cleared, ready for the electricians to do their work. The sudden change in temperature is unbelievable as you descend. Damp and dusty and full of junk, the cellars must have been an impressive sight in their day, full of hundreds, if not thousands, of bottles of fine wines and Champagnes.

It was the ideal place to get away from the hot summer sun and cool off for a while. In contrast, the electricians joked what bright spark decided to put us down here in the middle of one of the best summers we've had for years. To them, it was the worst possible place to work and break times would find them out in the gardens, sunning themselves, or having a quick dip in the pool if no one was around.

As always, nature seems to restore the balance and come September, the rains came. Lawns and fields that had looked dead began to recover, and within a few weeks were back to normal. Turf that had been unavailable for months was being sold again. Now we could get on with a backlog of landscaping work, and earn some money.

We had a contract with Condor Steel of Burton on Trent to landscape the grounds of their new headquarters. They had moved into the old railway station at Eggington Junction in Derbyshire. The work involved tree planting and the laying of thousands of square yards of turf, and was the largest landscape project we'd undertaken to date. After the drought, we now had to contend with water-logged ground and thick mud, and there was a deadline to meet. Luckily for us, Condor was a good company to work for and understood the horrendous conditions we were working under. Nevertheless, apart from a few minor items, the job was finished in time for the opening.

The Condor contract had kept us busy well into my second winter. It also paid well, and more importantly they paid on time, which was crucial to me in those early days, having so little capital. We couldn't afford to have large sums of money outstanding for long periods of time. Unfortunately, companies such as Condor turned out to be rare, and the future would teach us some hard lessons and show us just how difficult being in business can be, especially when it comes to money and getting paid. I've also learnt that contracts, more often than not, are not worth the paper they are written on.

It soon became clear to me that the key to building a successful business comes from reputation, recommendation and trust, of taking opportunities when they arise. This was certainly the case in those early days, when openings were few, and leads to new work were thin on the ground. The best help and advice came from people in the trade, the Collyers and Woodhouses, men who ran small businesses, well-respected family firms. Having worked all their lives, they now watched over a new generation, guiding them through the difficulties and pitfalls of running the family firm. Keeping a careful eye on everything and everyone around them.

They were serious plain-speaking men, looking you up and down, trying to weigh you up as a person. Old George at the GEM Concrete works was a man of few words, and as blunt as they come. My first encounter with him was a lesson in salesmanship itself, when I enquired after a particular type of slab. 'Don't have any,' he snapped. This was followed by silence. 'Well, will you be having any in?' 'Yes.' Silence. 'Err, any idea when?' 'No.' Silence. 'Shall I try later?' 'Up to you.' Silence. Perhaps he didn't like the look of me, I don't know, but it took some time to get to know him, unlike his son George Junior, who was a totally different personality. They were from an older generation, when times were hard; men who had built up their companies from nothing and had a lifetime of experience of who to trust and who not to trust. Fortunately they were willing to trust us, and give us credit. We, who had no reputation or experience in business, and like so many before, could have disappeared at any time, taking their money with us.

The Collyers are well known in the Derby area. They run a small nursery at Borrowash on the outskirts of Derby, and their help and advice in those early days was invaluable. The Woodhouses were market traders specialising in fresh flowers, fruit and vegetables. In 1952, Mr Woodhouse opened a small nursery and market garden at Findern near Derby. Growing and selling their own produce from a small shop on the premises, this small family-run business began to grow, and from those humble beginnings and with the help of his son Arnold, it developed into a modern-day garden centre. As well as having tireless energy, Arnold was a man with a vision, his dream being to create one of the best centres around. A relatively new concept in those early days, he soon realised that supplying everything the gardener could want under one roof was the way forward – a full range of goods and services. From the manager Peter Smith, Della on sales to Reg the yardman, Oakdale Nurseries soon became a byword for quality and service. And there is no better way of selling your wares than to display them at their best, and that's where we came in.

With no expense spared, Arnold gave us the job of creating his shop window, or in this case, the summer and winter planting schemes on display at the nursery's entrance. This made it one of the most attractive garden centres to visit. Constantly changing and reflecting each season, inspiring the customer, who needed little encouragement to buy. This was a shrewd investment on Arnold's part, resulting in more business, an ever-increasing turnover, which led to big investment and expansion.

Our work at the nursery resulted in many new customers, all recommended by Arnold and his family. We had enquiries for all types of work, from landscape to maintenance, carried out on gardens of every size and description.

One project took months to complete, and involved the planting of thousands of trees and shrubs imported from Holland to landscape the grounds of a new mansion built by Roger Bullivant over at Newton Solney near Repton. Then there was the man from Burton who was the first person to win a million pounds on the Pools. He served us tea in china cups on a silver tray, and just like a man who had just won a million pounds, didn't seem to have a care in the world. When I told him there was a problem with the sighting of his new garden path, in so much as there was a tree in the way, his reply was 'Don't tell me your troubles, kid, I've enough of my own!' as he walked off smiling to himself.

Due to Arnold's passion and dedication, Oakdale Nurseries became one of the best garden centres for miles around. His help and advice to me in those early days was all given free, without a hint of reward. One cannot put a price on friendship, but there is no doubt it helped us to survive those years. Arnold sold the business and retired. It is now part of a well-known chain of garden centres. Arnold's son Martin still runs a landscape supply business in Findern, close to the old family nursery; a company we have traded with since its beginnings, and still do to this day.

Things were looking up. With full order books, and making a reasonable profit, I now felt confident enough to approach the bank for a mortgage. We sat in silence, the manager studying the accounts, scrutinising every penny, where it came from and where it was spent. In those days, mortgages weren't given lightly, especially if you were self-employed, and I felt more like a bank robber than a prospective house buyer. At last he spoke. 'How much did you require, Mr Elliott?' 'Well, Kath and I do have a property in mind,' I said nervously. 'It's a three bedroomed semi, valued at £8000, and we do have a deposit.' There was silence again as he spent time with a calculator poring over the figures, giving me the occasional glance, as if trying to weigh up any potential risks to his money. Then to my relief he agreed, but added 'We shall require a twenty-five per cent deposit.' I was in shock. I expected ten or maybe even fifteen per cent, but twenty-five per cent was ridiculous. 'That's two thousand pounds!' I told him. 'That's the terms, so it's up to you!' he said, sitting there smugly waiting for my reply. Knowing it would almost wipe out the small amount of cash flow I had accumulated over the last few years, and put us back to square one financially, the offer was reluctantly accepted, but at least we were now going to own a house, and have a foot on the first rung of the property ladder.

So far I'd made do with part-time help. Old Fred had been with me from almost the beginning. With an ever-increasing workload, full-time labour was now a necessity, and with it came my first experience of the labour market. This was a daunting prospect for anyone not used to the ways of hiring employees. Instead of just informing the job centre of the vacancy, I naively placed an advert in the local newspaper. This resulted in what seemed like a million applicants for the job, ringing up at all hours of the day and night for days on end. Even with the vacancy filled, they would sometimes call at the house in person, still trying to convince me that they were the right person for the job. As in the past, some were good and some were bad. Some would stay for a long time, and some would arrive with great enthusiasm and then mysteriously disappear. Some were quite forgettable, while others would leave an impression that would last a lifetime.

We didn't realise it at the time, but those first few years had been a struggle. A struggle tempered only by our youth, enthusiasm and energy. Such was the need to carry on earning our daily crust, we didn't have time to dwell on the negative.

8

Into the Tomb

We approached the north gate at Kedleston Hall with some trepidation. The journey up from town had been full of laughter and bravado, joking amongst ourselves as to who should have the honour of flushing her out. Young Paul had already volunteered, but Fred insisted it must be me. After all, if she is a dragon like they say, George should be the man to do it.

The moment our tyres hit the gravel, a curtain flashed. She knew we'd arrived. We'd been warned. Woofy had been on the tom-toms the night before and his message was clear; don't mess with Madge, she's fierce, and whatever you do, be careful with those gates.

The new tenant at North Lodge had been over-zealous in her new role as guardian of the gates. This had already led to one or two near punch-ups with tenants and staff down at the hall, arguments about the way the heavy ornamental gates should be opened. Bear in mind they had been there for over 200 years, and must have been opened and closed a million times at least.

Not to be intimidated, our plan was to rattle them a little, and as Fred put it, flush her out to see what she's made of, to show her who's boss. All in good fun, of course.

Fred was smirking. 'Haven't you forgotten something?'

'Like what?'

'Like your sword.'

I gestured a polite sod off, and made my way towards the gate. As soon as my hand touched the latch her door was

open, only a few inches, but just enough for her peer out of the darkness and still remain unseen, waiting and watching my every move.

Perhaps it was the fear of the unknown, but my courage seemed to drain away. The thought of what might be lurking in the shadows made me tread with caution and leave it till another day. At this moment I didn't want to know. I opened the gates in my usual careful way. Her job done, she closed the door.

Then, as often happens, just as I am about to close up, someone else pulls up behind me to enter the park, and as manners dictate, I push back the gate to let them in, and BANG! It hit the buffer on the side of the lodge. She was out of her lair in a flash, like some black widow spider, ready to devour its next victim. I was caught in her web.

'MIND THE BLOODY GATES,' she snarled.

My decision not to provoke her had been a wise one, for there before me stood five foot nothing of raw intimidation. Small but well built, with the voice of a sergeant major, she was confident and fearless, and I knew she wouldn't take prisoners. Woofy was right; not a woman to mess with.

I squeaked a grovelled apology and left her, hands on hips, staring menacingly at her next victim waiting to enter the park while I legged it back to the van, there to be greeted by Fred and Paul, sitting there with stupid grins on their faces.

'Here you are,' said Fred, 'I told you to take your sword!' as he mockingly waving a rolled-up newspaper in my face.

Publicans by trade, Madge and her husband Sid used to run a thriving city-centre alehouse, and by all accounts, didn't have any trouble with the locals or with anybody else for that matter. Knowing Madge, I can see why.

They had moved to Kedleston to retire to a quieter life. Compared to the pub, it was quiet, but not for long.

Almost from day one she began to upset people. Most ignored her, but one unfortunate gentleman took matters a stage further by squaring up to Madge. Then things really got out of hand.

That was the day she locked horns with Freddy Fleetwood, the cook's husband.

The Fleetwoods lived in a ground floor flat in the stabling yard. She was cook to the Scarsdales; a pleasant and friendly woman. Whenever she saw us working by the family wing, a cup of tea was soon on its way. Not your usual cup of tea, but one like you've never seen before. When it first appeared we all thought it was April Fool's Day, and fell about laughing.

'This has got to be from the Mad Hatter's tea party!' I said in disbelief. With a teacup the size of a dogs bowl, it must have held a pint of tea at least, sitting on a saucer as big as a dinner plate. 'Lord Scarsdale won't get out of bed until he's drunk two of these with his breakfast every morning,' Mrs Fleetwood assured us.

Freddy Fleetwood passed through the north gate every day on his way to and from work. Always smartly dressed, he reminded me of Liberace, the famous pianist.

Perhaps he was just having a bad day. We may never know the reasons why Freddy decided to confront Madge on that fateful day.

They'd had words before, but this time after another unsavoury comment from Madge, Freddy was determined to have his say. A serious misjudgement on his part.

A blazing row ensued with both parties trading insults; this went on for some time. Freddy then made a big mistake. In the heat of the moment, he poked Madge in the chest. Her reaction was instant; her bar-keeping skills immediately came into play and she went for poor old Freddy sending him sprawling backwards onto the ground.

Fortunately for Madge, and to Freddy's credit, the incident was never reported. When Sid told me the story sometime later, I was curious to know why no one else knew about it.

'Well, think about it,' said Sid. 'Would you want the world to know that you had been humiliated by a poor defenceless old woman?'

He was grinning like the Cheshire Cat. I sat there listening, shaking my head in sympathy. Then the penny dropped – it was Madge he was talking about, and she was anything but a poor defenceless old woman. 'I'd rather go ten rounds with Muhammad Ali than tackle your Madge,' I told him, 'but I can see your point.' If word came out, Freddy would have never lived it down.

Madge and Freddy kept out of each other's way. Freddy's lesson was learnt, but it wasn't the case with Madge, who continued to rub people up the wrong way and didn't seem to care who it was.

One of the duties of the gatekeeper is to open the gates for the lord and lady. They normally signal their arrival with a polite toot on the horn when approaching. The Rt Hon Francis Curzon also expected the same respect; after all, he was to be the next Lord Scarsdale.

This annoyed Madge greatly. This was evident one morning as I drew up behind Mr Curzon's Jeep. He'd been waiting patiently for Madge to open up. Seeing who it was she took her time, too long in fact, prompting several prolonged blasts of the horn from a very irate Mr Curzon, until she eventually appeared. The pair exchanged venomous looks as he sped off down the drive, waved on with a parting gesture from Madge, which I can assure you wasn't a victory sign.

'One of these days I'm gonna shove that horn right up his arse,' she declared, as we passed through. We advised her to be careful; he is the next Lord Scarsdale and your future boss so be warned, we told her. Advice that I'm sure fell on deaf ears.

It took some time but she eventually mellowed, and we saw a softer side to her character. We looked after the lodge gardens, and tea with Madge became something to look forward to. Her Bakewell tart was without doubt the best on the planet, and her Siberian crab apple jelly second to none. If the weather was cold, she would invite us into her tiny little gatehouse. Cosy and warm, a spiral staircase gave access to the bedroom above. There they would both reminisce about the good old pub days. Telling tales of drunken barflies, and how Madge would deal with barroom brawlers, the sound of her rasping voice and her menacing stare were enough to send the hardest of men running for the door, Sid told us. They had enough stories to fill a book. But the future wasn't far off and changes were coming sooner than we thought down at the hall.

It was unusual for Madge to come out and open the gates. She looked upset, with tears in her eyes. Oh no, I thought, she's thumped someone again and been sacked. We pulled up to hear the bad news.

'The lord's fell off his perch,' she cried.

'He's what?' Madge's use of the English language was as colourful as ever.

'He's snuffed it.'

'What do you mean, snuffed it?'

'Are ya deaf or daft or what? He's dead, in other words. As dead as a door nail. They found him this morning; he must have died in his sleep.'

It was 19 October 1977 when Richard Nathaniel Curzon, second Viscount Scarsdale, passed away aged 79. For fifty-two of those years he had been Lord of Kedleston, and now there was to be a grand funeral.

On our way down to the hall Fred seemed to be in pain, his face contorted, then his shoulders began to shake. He was almost in tears.

'Something's tickled him,' said Paul. 'He's laughing.'

'I've just had a vision,' said Fred. 'I could see old Joe, who stands on the corner of the market hall selling the *Telegraph*. Imagine his sales pitch tomorrow. "Extra, extra, read all about it, the lord's snuffed it and fell of his perch"!'

Much water has flowed under the Adam Bridge since I first set eyes on the Kedleston estate. The drive down to the hall never disappoints, filling our senses with the glorious sights and sounds of autumn. Flights of Canada geese passed above us, skimming the treetops, winging their way down to the lakes to join the hundreds already there. The park was alive with squawking, squabbling and cackling. In more ways than one, Duck City was waking to a new dawn.

There was already a lot of activity over at the east wing with people coming and going, paying their respects. Woofy was on tenterhooks. He was still a little shocked, as it was he and the butler who had found his Lordship dead in bed that morning. He was telling us how his Lordship departed this world.

'Just as he came in,' he said, 'in his birthday suit.'

He'd had his orders and there was much to do. The gardens and churchyard would have to be spruced up, and seating for hundreds would have to be arranged ready for the grand occasion. Our first job was to help the estate men move several items from the church over to the Marble Hall where the service was to be held – a job that was easier said than done. The weight of the lectern was unbelievable and carrying it through the chapel garden to the hall, which was some distance, nearly gave us all a hernia.

We set about tidying the grounds; autumn in the garden can be a messy time. With the October winds and leaves everywhere, it was an almost impossible task, but we made a reasonable job of it.

'There's a problem over at the church, and they need your help.'

It was the familiar voice of Roy Adams. The one-time butler now seemed to be helping out on the estate. The part didn't suit him; he looked like a fish out of water. I was more used to seeing him immaculately dressed in his butler's outfit. He had been drafted in along with the rest of us in preparation for the big day.

Roy had been with the family for years. He lived in the village with his wife, Betty. Quiet and softly spoken, our paths crossed many times over the years. I found him to be a cultured man, but always rather serious. His knowledge of the house and its family history was second to none. He had a passion for antiques and restoration. His dream was to open an antiques shop one day.

On our way to the church, Roy seemed in a pensive mood, deep in thought. 'What does the future hold for us I wonder, now that the old boy's gone? Perhaps I should have a go at renting a shop, and make a new start. You did it, didn't you?' he asked.

'Yes, and I have no regrets, Roy, but until you try you will never know. Just go were your heart takes you.'

We had to call in at the gun room, to pick up some sort of implement required in the church. The gun room was to be found somewhere in the depths of the hall. A fascinating place, crammed full of everything the seasoned hunter could want. A battered old table took centre stage, used for preparing and repairing equipment. It was full of gun parts, fishing reels, nets, lines and bits of old rods, almost anything to do with shooting and fishing. Odd bits of armaments hung on the walls and on top of gun cabinets.

'I bet some of this stuff has been here for years,' I said to Roy, 'handed down over the centuries.'

'Yes, it may well have been,' he said, 'but whatever you do, don't touch anything, and I mean anything. I've learnt from past experience, if there's the slightest thing out of place, he'll know about it.'

A few seconds passed before Roy realised what he'd just said. He looked at me and we both smiled.

I said 'I think you're right, Roy,' and he nodded. He was probably looking down on us right then. So I left well alone.

Some years later whilst browsing through an antiques shop in Derbyshire, Roy appeared from the back room. Did he fulfil his dream? I don't know, but it was good to see him again and talk about old times.

He wrote a book about his life and times at Kedleston. Almost from day one it seemed to tell a sad tale, a story of a man full of bitterness and regret.

Was this the Roy I knew? I hope not. I still find it hard to believe he spent twenty-five years of his life working in misery, having little time for his colleagues, apart from the odd one or two, blaming his misfortune on a band of gypsies who turned up at the Hall centuries ago begging for food and water. After being turned away, it was said they put a curse on the Curzons, and all who work for them, but I think not. I'm afraid the myth of the gypsy's curse remains just that; a myth.

First recorded in 1198, the Norman south doorway is all that remains of the original church. The main body of All Saints today dates back to the thirteenth century. It is the last remaining part of the old village of Kedleston, which was moved about a mile to the west in 1757.

It's one of my favourite places. Many are the times when I have sat in quiet contemplation within its cool walls, resting from the summer heat. There are dozens of monuments to the Curzon family throughout the church. These make interesting reading. They range from medieval effigies to neo-classical tombs, the earliest being that of Thomas De Curzon, who died in 1245.

In the churchyard, all the headstones are laid flat. This makes for easy reading for someone mowing up and down the rows. At one time I could remember the names off by heart, the Salts and Yates, I would have loved to know who they were and how they lived. What happened to Ann Appleyard, who was only twenty? Why did she die at such a young age?

Woofy was waiting inside the church along with George Tongue. George and his father carried out building maintenance on the estate.

'Someone's been checking out the tomb ready for the funeral,' said George, 'and there's a problem; the winding gear isn't working. We have to go down and try and fix it.'

'We're stumped,' said Woofy. 'If we can't get it to work, we'll have to bump him feet first down the spiral staircase, and that won't be a pretty sight.'

The tomb and memorial chapel was built by Lord Curzon in memory of his first wife, Mary Leiter, who died in 1906. George

Nathaniel Curzon, the first Marquis of Kedleston, was born in 1859. The former Viceroy of India was the most famous Curzon of them all. He was a brilliant man who held high rank in public life for more than a generation, holding the office of foreign secretary. He was leader of the House of Lords until his death in 1925. They say his greatest disappointment was never becoming prime minister.

A beautiful white marble sculpture depicting the effigies of Lord and Lady Curzon lies above the tomb. Serene and exquisite in every detail, it's surrounded by a green marble floor, which reflects a soft glowing light from lovely stained glass windows. The chapel is a must-see for any visitor to Kedleston.

There are two ways to enter the tomb. One is through a small door in the corner of the chapel that leads to a spiral staircase. The other is via the chapel floor itself.

Designed to be lowered using a winding mechanism, the coffin is placed on a platform in the marble floor which conveys the casket into the tomb below. And this is where the problem was; it hadn't been used in years and had seized up. It had to be fixed, and quick. Used on the day of the service, it was the only way the coffin could be committed to the ground.

We entered the tomb. A damp fusty smell hung in the air as we peered around in the dim light. Something scurried across the floor and up the wall, heading towards the air vents. We made our way to the centre of the chamber.

'Good heavens,' cried Woofy, 'I thought this place was built just for the Viceroy and his missus, but it looks like they're all here, generations of them.'

All round the tomb lay the lords and ladies of Kedleston from centuries past, sleeping peacefully, awaiting that final Day of Judgement.

A few vacant spaces remained, ready for their descendents.

The Viceroy and Lady Mary took pride of place in the centre of the tomb, directly below the marble sculpture, their coffins grand, more ornate and colourful than the others, reflecting the stature of the man who built it.

George beckoned us over to one of the empty compartments.

'Look at this lads, old Dick booked his place years ago, here's his reservation.'

There, on the back an old cigarette packet, he'd written the words 'Reserved for Richard Nathaniel Curzon' and the date, 1960-something. George set about trying to fix the winding gear while Woofy and I poked around, fascinated by the whole experience. Some of the coffins were a little the worse for wear. Split and cracked, they were obviously centuries old.

Then Woofy spotted a small box.

'This one must have been a music lover,' he said. 'He's brought along his violin.'

His comment brought a swift rebuke from George, who told him his joke was in bad taste, but Woofy looked puzzled, and he wasn't joking. To his embarrassment, he didn't realise that small box was in fact an infant's coffin. The contraption, as Woofy called it, seemed to be fixed. It was time to try it out.

'Just how heavy are these coffins?' asked George.

We tried in vain to move one. They must have been half a ton at least. It was decided he and Woofy should go up top, to add as much weight as possible to the platform. I was to stay below to lower them down. Standing alone in the tomb was an eerie experience. I tried desperately not to look around, concentrating on the job in hand, but couldn't resist the odd glance over my shoulder, peering goggle-eyed into darkest corners of the tomb, half expecting to see something move.

'We're ready!' shouted George.

I began to wind them down. The floor came down slowly. A dazzling light came flooding into the tomb, illuminating every corner, sending the resident spiders running for cover. Two pairs of workman's socks came in to view as they made their descent. The platform came down about a foot, and then it jammed. With a little more tweaking and a drop more oil, I tried again. This time it came down a little lower, but jammed again.

This went on for some time; the tomb bathed in bright light

one minute, and plunged into darkness the next. The constant switch from light to dark began to affect my eyes. Each time the floor closed up, it took time for my eyes to adjust and for just a few seconds, there was total darkness and weird shapes flickered in front of me. I tried to convince myself that it was just my imaginings; it was just the light playing tricks with my eyes, but it didn't help when the cracks on some of the older coffins seemed to be getting wider.

While I was winding Woofy and George up and down, they were doing their best to wind me up in return, making conversation just loud enough for me to hear.

'Did you see something down there, Woofy?' said George.

'Yes, it was over in the corner, but I didn't want to say anything. It had big teeth though.'

My imagination was running wild as they continued their wicked comments. Now those flickering lights seemed to take shape and form. My thoughts drifted back to my youth when, for a laugh, a group of friends and I set out to contact the dead, and got more than we bargained for. It was back in the sixties, and Miss Crossley had died. She lived in the big house at Priory Flatte near the village of Breadsall. The house had stood empty and neglected for some time. It was said to be haunted by the ghost of Miss Crossley's long lost love who had died before they could marry. It all began in fun, when a group of us decided to find out for ourselves if the rumours were true. Laughing and joking we made our way into the house through an open window and settled down for the night in an oak-panelled room. The gas, water and electricity had been cut off so the place was pitch black. All we had was one small torch between us. We joked nervously amongst ourselves, trying to scare each other to death. It was well into the night before we finally drifted off to sleep. Then it happened, boom! We awoke, cursing and swearing, the torch flashing from one face to another to see who the culprit was, but it was evident from the wide eyes and startled looks that this was no joke. Before we could settle, it happened again and continued throughout the night. Sleep was impossible, as we began to wonder if there really was a ghost trying to figure out a way to make contact. This came in the way of questions, answered by a sound that could be felt rather than heard, a sort of code. Throughout that long summer people came to listen, and attempts were made to uncover what many thought to be a hoax, but no one could, and so it remained a mystery. The big house was eventually sold and turned into a training centre for the water industry. In 1997 it was sold again and then finally demolished to make way for a new housing estate. That's where I now live, just a hundred yards from where the old haunted house used to stand. Even now, after all those years, what happened then made me realise anything is possible.

Being alone in the tomb, I still expected to hear that old familiar booming sound from the past, trying desperately to keep calm, but as the platform closed up, I felt as if Dracula himself was coming out of the shadows, moving across the tomb behind me, and then I'd start winding furiously to reopen it, hoping the light would send him flying back to his box before he could sink his teeth into the back of my neck.

The problem seemed to take an age to fix and then, with some relief, I made my way out of the tomb.

'By heck,' said Woofy, 'you look like you've just seen a ghost.'

'Why didn't one of you give me a hand?' I complained.

'We thought about it, but you seemed to be coping quite well without us,' he said, smiling away in great amusement.

The funeral took place amongst the splendour of the Marble Hall, its twenty-five foot pink alabaster columns providing a grand setting for a grand send off. Attended by the great and the good, the service was conducted by the Bishop of Derby. Lady Scarsdale invited me to the service. I was touched, until she asked if I would be kind enough to help Woofy out with the car parking arrangements. I didn't really mind. A few honoured guests were allowed through the main gates. Mostly close friends and family, with the odd celebrity or two, Lady Isobel Barnett being one of the last to arrive.

With everyone inside, Woofy and I made our way up the steps to the Marble Hall, only to have the doors closed in our faces. The place was full. After the service, and with all the pomp and ceremony befitting a peer of the realm, Richard Nathaniel Curzon was laid to rest in the family tomb.

It was rumoured the winding gear failed again during the interment service and had to be fixed. It may have been the reason why the coffin was damaged. Some time later, George Tongue had the unenviable task of being present while his Lordship's body was removed, and the coffin resealed.

The late lord's wife became Dowager Lady Scarsdale. After a period of grace, she moved to Oxfordshire to live with her son. On 7 June 1978 we all attended a farewell party. It was held in Caesar's Hall, where she was presented with a painting of Kedleston before giving a final and emotional farewell speech.

Lord Scarsdale's funeral was the first I'd ever been to but, by pure coincidence, on the very day I attended the grand ceremony at the hall, my grandmother Kate died. Now I had to attend her funeral just a few days later. The contrast between the two couldn't have been more apparent, reflecting the way they lived their lives. They were about the same age and lived just a few miles apart, but that's where the similarity ends. Born at opposite ends of the social scale, their journeys though life had been on totally different paths and both would have different crosses to bear.

The lord, whose life had been one of privilege and wealth, was a man of the world and of influence; master of all he surveyed, and with the power to shape the lives of people around him. He lived in one of England's finest houses, set in the heart of a great estate. He would spend a lifetime trying to hold on to what the Curzons held, (this is the family motto), preserving a way of life with an uncertain future, a custodian of a great house with all its history, traditions, worries and responsibilities. His noble ancestry can be traced back centuries. He departed this world in style, with a following of hundreds, a ceremony remembered for its pomp and splendour. He now rests in his own private family tomb, surrounded by his ancestors.

My grandmother Kate, mother and housewife, had a life of scrimping and scraping and watching every penny. She lived all her life in a small rented house, and never saw anything of the world around her, rarely travelling from her home town. She made a promise to us all. When my boat comes in, you'll want for nothing. Her boat did come in, albeit a small one. After being left a small legacy by a brother, she promptly gave it all away to her children and grandchildren. Her needs were few. She would spend the last thirty years of her life trekking across town visiting a hospitalised son damaged by war. Her noble ancestry also goes back centuries, but to where, we'll never know.

Her departure from this life was marked by a simple ceremony, attended by barely half a dozen family members, but it will always be remembered for its laughter when a rather large vicar came sweeping into the chapel to conduct the service. This prompted a rather unflattering comment from Uncle Reg, who cried out

'He likes his grub!' The small family gathering fell about in fits of laughter, which continued throughout the service. The vicar was oblivious to it all; he didn't realise we were laughing at him. He even congratulated us for being such a happy bunch.

'This is how it should be,' he said. 'A time to celebrate a life, not one of gloom and doom,' and he thanked us all for making it such a joyous occasion. Unlike his Lordship, Kate now rests with the multitudes in Nottingham Road cemetery.

Looking down on Kate's grave for the last time, I stood alone deep in thought. At least they are equal now, and perhaps in the next life the cards may be dealt differently. Maybe. Who knows? Then my thoughts went back to the churchyard at Kedleston, and to the grave of William Smith who died in 1878. His prophetic message to us all is to be found written on his gravestone:

> Remember, man, as you pass by,
> As you are now, so once was I,
> As I am now, so must you be,
> Prepare yourself to follow me.

A sober remainder to us all that eternity is just over the horizon and could arrive at any time.

9

Changes at the Hall

The recession-hit economy of the early 1980s brought with it high levels of unemployment, especially amongst the youth. Desperate efforts were made by the government to create jobs. Various schemes, such as YTS, designed to give the young a chance in the workplace by subsidising employers to take them on. For a miserly twenty-three pounds, fifty pence a week, it was a source of cheap labour for some unscrupulous employers. With business doing well, I now employed several people. Kath and I had been lucky with our first house. Prices had doubled in just four years; we were able to afford a bigger mortgage and move to a new house.

We were often approached by the local employment office, eager to get someone off their books and into a trade. 'We have a young lad called Chalky who's hardworking and willing to learn. He's already had a number of jobs, so he does have some experience.' 'What happened to the other jobs?' I enquired. 'Well, some of them were temporary, and others just unsuitable.' I was a little doubtful, but decided to give him a chance.

Throughout history, great minds have come to the fore helping us to understand the universe and the world around us; da Vinci, Newton, Einstein, all great men, ahead of their time, a rare breed of genius. There are leaders and politicians, the clever and not so clever, who go to make up this complex and wonderful race called mankind. And then there's Chalky. In the unlikely event of an alien invasion, I pray Chalky is the first to be taken.

The world would then be safe, as I'm in no doubt that after a few minutes' interrogation, they would beam him straight back to Earth again sending orders to the fleet to stay well clear of that little blue planet at all costs. Has he a great mind? No. Unique? Yes. Is he ahead of his time? Sometimes he is, and sometimes he's behind. Chalky's interpretation of time itself would have sent even the great Isaac Newton rushing for his charts and books in disbelief. A great orator? No. A talker? Yes. If it ever became an Olympic sport, Chalky could talk for England and bag gold every time. He could certainly give any of the world's great speakers a run for their money in the talking department. Whether or not they could understand what he was babbling on about is a different matter.

Chalky was a southerner, having moved up with his parents from Ashford in Kent. It took me all of two minutes to realise that Chalky didn't have any work experience at all – not in the true sense of the word, that is. Personality-wise, Chalky was a real bright spark, cheerful and polite, but his work experience amounted to nothing and there was a serious downside to his character, his mouth; he wouldn't stop talking.

I soon realised this was the cause of his problems. Chalky talked so much, he didn't have time to listen. In fact, he'd gone through most of his short life without listening too much at all, hence his inability to hold down a proper job, but I liked him and looked on him as a bit of a challenge, and what a challenge it would turn out to be!

'If you're going to do the job, I want it doing right.' I'd told Chalky for the umpteenth time to sweep the drive again, and this time to do it properly. It was only mid morning, and he was already trying my patience. I needed a drink. I sent him over to the van to check the time. Chalky came back with a puzzled look on his face and stood there in silence. 'Well, go on, what time is it then?' 'It's about ten past quarter past ten.' 'Ten past quarter past what?' I asked in disbelief. That's when my Oliver Hardy look was born, just like Ollie in those old Laurel and Hardy films after his sidekick made some daft remark. I stood there, staring blankly into space, unable to comprehend what I'd just heard. 'I don't know,' said Chalky, 'that's what it looks like to me. It's one of those clocks with hands on it, and I'm not very good with them.' Chalky had been brought up on digital, and just read out the numbers. Unbelievably, he had never learnt or been taught to tell the time. After decoding his interpretation of time, it was quite simple. Ten past quarter past ten was in fact, twenty-five minutes past ten. Just as ten past a quarter to eleven was five to eleven, and half past twenty past two is ten minutes to three. Simple.

I pulled him up yet again about his work. Slow down Chalky, you cannot sweep fifty yards of path in two minutes. That was it. His brush went into the air and he stormed off. It was plain to see why he couldn't hold down a job. At the first sign of criticism he was off, and he must have taken a lot in his short working life – and not only criticism. His naivety and outgoing personality must have left him open to bullies, pranksters and mickey-takers. Walking out was his defence mechanism.

I felt disappointed to say the least, and also a bit of a failure. I felt sure that given the time and a little encouragement, we could have made something of him. I thought I'd heard the last of him, but I was wrong. That evening his father rang, demanding to know what had happened. He began ranting and raving about the way I'd treated poor old Chalky. How I made his life a misery, by making him sweep the paths again and again. The man was non-stop; I couldn't get a word in edgeways. Chalky was certainly a chip off the old block, I thought. Finally, I managed to butt in and try to explain the problem. 'He has to learn to do it properly,' I said. He was off again, screaming down the phone. 'Are you telling me our Chalky doesn't know how to sweep up?' 'No he doesn't, and to be honest, he doesn't know how to do much at all.' 'Like what?' he stormed. 'Well, for starters, he can't even tell the time. 'Don't talk daft,' he said. 'Look, all I want is his for him to learn to do the job properly.' 'What you want, mate, is a punch up the frote,' he said, 'and I'm just the one to do it.' The man was almost calling me a bully, and that really annoyed me. 'Right, that's it!' I shouted. 'I'm coming down to your house, and we can sort this out face to face!' The phone went dead, and I knew that would be the end of the matter for now.

The next day the man from the employment office was on the phone. 'I owe you an apology,' he said. 'I should have warned you about Chalky and told you what to expect. He's asked for another chance, and his dad has also apologised for his outburst on the phone.' 'I'll take him back under one condition.' 'What's that?' 'That he stops talking, and starts listening.'

After a little encouragement, Chalky realised that not everyone in the world was against him, and he soon settled in. He became a useful member of the team and the customers seemed to like him, although trying to put an end to his rabbiting was an impossible task. I'd have more chance of parting the Red Sea. His customary greeting of 'I'm the man from Kent' also had to be discouraged. 'Well, I am the man from Kent!' he said, looking a little indignant. I tried to explain. 'It's the word "Kent", Chalky, it must be your accent, but it sounds like another word that isn't very flattering.' Chalky wasn't bothered, and continued with his 'I'm the man from Kent' greeting. 'Yes and I can see why', often came the reply.

With the death of the old lord, change came to the hall. A new era was underway at Kedleston, and with it came a new gardener, Jeff Waples, the walking tool bag. The new head gardener had arrived from Chesterfield, and for the first time in many years the grounds had a real gardener in charge. 'Real' as in professional. Jeff was the typical old-fashioned type, and certainly dressed for the part with his collar, tie and gardener's apron. It had a very large pocket, bulging with tools, string and wire – almost everything apart from the kitchen sink. With a vast knowledge of horticulture, what Jeff didn't know he could soon find out from the library of magazines, catalogues and books he kept in the gardener's shed. He

could also talk; not in the same league as Chalky, but close. Once again we were invited to the Hall, This time to a welcoming party. The late Lord's cousin and heir, Frances Curzon, the third Viscount Scarsdale, had now moved in with his wife Lady Helene and their two young sons, Richard and James. They occupied the twenty-three roomed east wing of the hall. The Curzon boys were always well mannered and polite, and at every opportunity they would be out in the garden. Their first objective would be the old Ferguson tractor and me. With them on board, hanging on for dear life, we would race around the gardens on imaginary journeys to who knows where, shooting imaginary bullets at who knows what.

With a new era comes new ideas, and we all knew it wouldn't be long before Lord and Lady Scarsdale would begin leaving their own imprint on this historic house and garden. Having worked on their garden at Western Lodge, and knowing Lady Helene's appetite for a new challenge, I knew she would soon be putting her own ideas into place.

Designed by Lady Helene there was to be a new garden at the east wing. With an impressive knowledge of gardening, she knew exactly how to create the garden she wanted. Lady Helene is a woman of many talents. She has a charming personality that makes you feel at ease. But be warned, she also possesses tireless energy. Energy, when unleashed, goes though a garden like a tornado and I speak from experience when I say her enthusiasm has no bounds. She had a natural gift when it came to the composition and design of a garden; the manicured regimentation of the formal garden is not for her.

The east wing garden was a blank canvas – all lawn, apart from the odd rhododendron or two. A large beech tree stood at the far end. It was already sixty feet high when it was planted in the eighteenth century, after being transplanted from another part of the estate. This was a common practice years ago. On the great estates, when time and manpower was plentiful, even fully mature trees could be moved to create an instant effect on the garden or landscape.

Several new flowerbeds had to be prepared, ready for the many trees and shrubs her Ladyship had chosen for her new garden. Preparation is usually a simple process that involves taking off the turf and digging over. It became anything but simple. A few inches down, we came across the remains of some old buildings, conveniently swept under the carpet centuries ago, ready for future generations of gardeners to break their backs on digging them out again. They could have possibly been from the old house, demolished to make way for the present hall, on which work began in 1759, or part of the original village. Who knows?

We began to uncover old brick pathways and floors. One or two old coins were found, together with bits of wire and old nails, even the remains of a fireplace, with ash still inside. What had started as a routine job now became a mini-archaeological dig and a lot of hard work, but very interesting. Barrow loads of old bricks had to be dug out before planting could commence. Most of them came out fairly easily, apart from one section that must have been a corner of the building; it wouldn't budge. Taking it in turns, we began the laborious job of trying to dislodge it with a hammer and chisel. Progress was slow, so Chalky decided a different method was called for. 'What it needs is some welly!' he cried, as he picked up a fourteen-pound sledgehammer and leapt into the hole. 'Watch out, he's been FINCKING again,' said Fred, mocking Chalky's Southern accent. Everyone scattered as he steadied himself for the decisive blow. He swung the hammer with all his might, hitting the side of the brickwork with a dull thud. You could almost feel the shockwaves as they reverberated through his body. For a few seconds, he stood motionless; we half expected him to disintegrate and fall to the floor in a pile of dust like the cartoon cat in *Tom and Jerry*. 'This FING must be FREE FOOT FICK!' cried Chalky, as he steadied himself for another blow, which we quickly discouraged.

We all hoped and prayed that Chalky and Waples would have something in common. Some mutual interest or subject they could discuss, so they could talk to each other, saving us all from the constant 'yak yak yak' at break times. As Fred put it, it was like being in a parrot house. I always vowed that next time, I would have my snap in the summerhouse. Waples' enthusiasm knew no bounds and he took every opportunity he could to talk to his Lordship, to discuss new ideas and projects, or more often than not just talk.

The constant attention from Waples became an irritation to his Lordship, who once asked me if everyone in Derbyshire suffered from verbal diarrhoea. 'I cannot walk in my own garden without being hit by a flood of it from Waples,' he said. 'Even if he's on the other side of the garden, he'll find some excuse to drop what he's doing and come scurrying across to greet me.'

With the new garden finished, Waples took responsibility for the watering. This was immediately taken over by his Lordship, who wanted to do his bit, but we all knew the real reason why he volunteered his services for what could be a time consuming job. The thought of being greeted by Waples every morning, with hosepipe in hand, must have been too much for his Lordship to bear. Even so, Waples still managed to upset him. This led to a confrontation in the gardener's shed that could have seen the end of us all.

Waples had lost the nozzle off the end of his hosepipe, so he decided to go over to the family wing and borrow his Lordship's. Not a good idea, especially when he forgot to tell him. Thinking he had lost the nozzle himself, his Lordship spent a considerable time looking for it, searching amongst the newly planted beds and borders. Then after a fruitless search, he was told by one of his sons that Waples had nicked it. He was furious, and took off after him.

Unfortunately we were all sitting in the gardener's shed at the time having our lunch break so we couldn't hear him ranting, raving and shouting for Waples as he searched all over the grounds. He was now going demented and when he checked out the last place Waples could be, the gardener's shed, he burst through the door spitting blood.

'Waples, where's my nozzle?' he stormed. Fred, who immediately saw the funny side of the situation, muttered under his breath. 'Just below your eyes, my lord.' My blood ran cold; this is it I thought, after nearly twenty years at the hall we were out. Did Fred really mishear him, thinking he'd said 'snozzel?' Knowing Fred, I don't think so. Now his mischievous wit was about to sink us all.

'WHAT DID YOU SAY?' His Lordship now turned his wrath on Fred. There was a deathly silence as he eyed him with suspicion, still unsure of what he'd heard. No one dared say a word, not even Chalky, who sat wide-eyed and speechless – a miracle in itself. We waited to hear how Fred could get us out of this one. Thankfully, as well as being a joker, Fred was extremely quick-witted and without a pause answered his Lordship with 'It's there before your eyes, my Lord,' pointing to an old sprinkler hanging on the wall. 'Not that you fool!' shouted his Lordship. The distraction was just enough for him to turn his attention back to a now petrified Waples, and to our great relief, he ordered him out of the shed to find the elusive nozzle.

The National Trust was the name on everyone's lips. Soon they would be taking over at Kedleston. This would mean changes not only for me, but also for one or two other people who lived at the hall. The Picards had lived in the China Flat for years. Their ground floor apartments were located in the main body of the hall itself, next to the Indian museum. Mr Picard's access to his flat was a little unusual to say the least; he always left his window open so he could climb in and out, saving him the time and trouble of making his way through the hall itself. To see two wiry legs appearing or disappearing through the open window was a comical sight.

A butcher by trade, he was a jovial character who always seemed to be smiling and whenever he saw me out on the tractor, there would always be a refreshing drink on its way. But I soon learned to taste it first. The first time I drank one of his concoctions, I thought I'd taken a funny turn as I drove like a drunkard across the great lawn, nearly driving the old Ferguson tractor over the ha-ha and into the field. What seemed like a nice refreshing drink of lemonade with ice and lemon turned out to be a cocktail of gin, tonic and Bacardi rum, and no half measures! The mowing was abandoned, and a quiet spot found to lie down and sleep it off.

Old Tommy Morris also became a victim some time later, when he unwittingly drank one of Picard's potions. Again it involved the old Ferguson tractor. This time, the consequences could have been more serious. As Tom mowed the lawns one day, he was blissfully unaware of the potency of Picard's brew until he tried to steer the tractor between two conifer trees at the far corner of the great lawn. With the booze taking effect, he must have been seeing double when he misjudged the gap between the two. He knocked one of them down; it fell on to the mower trailing behind, luckily bringing the tractor to halt only feet from the edge of a seven-foot drop.

The Picards moved from the hall to a small cottage owned by the estate. Roses and honeysuckle covered its walls; the garden was delightful, a typical cottage garden with a small vegetable plot and fruit orchard, in stark contrast to the grandeur of the hall, and a challenge to the Picards who now had to think about gardening for the first time. 'I know nothing at all about gardening,' he said, 'but if you can tidy it up, we should be able to manage.' Declining the offer of a refreshing drink, we settled for the more mundane tea and coffee until the work was finished. 'Come into the house, and I'll settle up with you,' said Mr Picard. I was still trying to work out my costs, when he came out of the kitchen carrying two bags. 'This should cover it,' he said, as he pulled out pound after pound of pork chops, sausages, bacon and beef.

Workers on great estates such as Kedleston were usually looked after on retirement, often allowed to stay in their cottages to live out the rest of their days. People like Tommy Brown and the old estate manager, Mr Walters. Mr Walters was a fine old gentleman who had given a lifetime of service to the Scarsdales. The estate built a bungalow in Kedleston village for him to live in. We had the pleasure of working on his garden. As he grew old, his garden became too much for him to manage, so we had the job of creating a new lawn. Mr Walters could take you back in time to another age; an age long gone. He used to talk of the old days, when he was in charge and as he put it, 'when the estate was alive.' When he first came to Kedleston, he could hire a housemaid for just a few pounds a year. Back in the 1920s, the wage bill for the whole estate only came to £45 a week, '...and I had nearly twenty people on the books then!' he would say. In those days people like Tommy Brown would be earning the princely sum of 7/6 a day, less than 40 pence a day in today's money. He spoke with affection about the lords and ladies he'd known, and how many he'd seen come and go in a lifetime at Kedleston.

Ken Woof and some of the other old hands had also retired. Roy Adams wife died, and he remarried some years later. Ken and his wife Eileen decided to make a clean break and move away from the hall. They had spent all their lives in tied accommodation, living in some of the most beautiful places up and down the country. Now they were about to move again for what would probably be their last time. Unable to buy a house, the only option was to rent. They found a small flat in a nice area of the city. It was a world away from that they had been used to, but with friends and family close by, they soon settled in. Ken and Eileen had become good friends, and over the years we always kept in touch.

The hall gardens have also undergone many changes since the National Trust took over in 1987. Gone are the shrubberies laid out by Mrs Player. The rose garden, a feature for many years, has now been ripped out and turfed over, and the swimming pool with its surrounding rose-clad columns is no longer there.

Over twenty years have passed since I first set eyes on the Kedleston estate. The estate had been a big part of my life, but now the National Trust were firmly in place and my relationship with the Curzon family, the hall and its lovely gardens would soon be changing.

On the last day, I decided to walk from North Lodge down to the hall. It was a misty autumn morning as I made my through the park, stopping for a few minutes on the edge of the woodland, as I had done all those years ago with my old boss Mick. I began to reflect on my time at Kedleston. Although I'd only had a taste of life on a great estate, it has left me with some wonderful memories of a bygone age, and of people who are no longer with us. For hundreds of years, the great house and estate have been passed down through the generations, but now the words of the family motto 'Let Curzon Hold What Curzon Held', wouldn't ring quite true. The National Trust had now taken over the hall and parkland in lieu of death duties, but the family would stay in their ancestral home, the east wing.

Now there would be changes, but when one door shuts, another one opens, or shuts in your face – or so the saying goes. After Kedleston, there were still many new doors to open. The one at the hall didn't close completely and I would be going back for many years to come to work on the gardens of the east wing for Lord and Lady Scarsdale. The garden they created has now matured. With a variety of trees, shrubs, bulbs, perennials and creepers on the walls, the garden is now an interesting addition to Kedleston. After the death of her husband, Frances, Lady Scarsdale moved to the Old Rectory in the village, a fine Georgian red brick house. This building had been part of the original village close to where the hall now stands. At a cost of £200 it was moved brick by brick back in the seventeenth century. There, with her usual expertise, she set about designing and creating a delightful new garden from a virtual wilderness. Her Ladyship's garden at Kedleston is now enjoyed by another young Curzon family. Richard Curzon, the young lad who along with his brother, used to ride on the old Ferguson tractor with me as we rode through the gardens all those years ago, now lives in the east wing, continuing the work of that distinguished family.

10

Danger in the Garden

The book made interesting and somewhat amusing reading. Question; How did the accident happen? Answer: Fell down a manhole. Question; Why did the accident happen? Answer: Because some idiot didn't fix the lid, and I fell in.

Look through the accident book on any building site and you will be reminded of the dangers and pitfalls of working in the construction industry. It serves as a warning to the unwary and the unprepared.

Although a totally different environment, the dangers of working in the peace and tranquillity of the English garden shouldn't be underestimated. Apart from the obvious risks posed by the use of tools, machinery and pesticides, the gardener has another foe waiting in the wings, Mother Nature herself. At any time, she can inflict pain, injury and disease on the unsuspecting from any source she chooses, from the largest living things on the planet to the smallest of creatures, organisms invisible to the naked eye, to the weather, with its storms, gales and lightning strikes and extremes of heat and cold. The peaceful English garden can be a deceptively dangerous place.

Without doubt, the biggest threat to life and limb over the years has come from one of the most majestic of all God's creations: trees. There have been many close encounters with them over the years, some too close for comfort. Perhaps I should have heeded old Harry's warning all those years ago; 'Don't mess with the trees!' We were only kids when we first met Harry. We awoke one morning to find ourselves staring into the barrel of a twelve bore shotgun as we unwittingly pitched our tent in his field, flattening his freshly-mown grass. He was the gardener-cum-farmhand and sometimes gamekeeper who worked for Miss Crossley at Priory Flatte, a small estate at Breadsall, close to where we lived. He was also a countryman, the first countryman we ever knew; a man who appreciated nature and the wonderful things around him.

As we grew up, we got to know him well. They were magical times for us, and out of those happy days of roaming the fields and woods of our childhood came a passion for the countryside, and with it a lifelong interest in trees. I was carving my name on the trunk of an old beech tree in Bluebell Wood when Harry came by with his warning; 'How would you like to be chopped at?' he said. 'I didn't take you for a tree hugger, Harry,' I said in fun, but he was serious. 'Just don't damage the trees,' he said. 'Mark my words; if you ever have anything to do with trees in the future, make sure you treat them with respect, or you'll be sorry.' He was right, and from time to time, Harry's words still come echoing down the decades.

Some of the oldest trees in Europe are to be found in Britain, with many fine specimens growing in the parks and great estates of Derbyshire. A solitary veteran stands in a churchyard at Darley Dale. Around 2000 years old, this ancient yew tree has a girth of 33 feet, and stood witness to the Roman occupation of Britain. The famous Major Oak in Sherwood Forest in Nottinghamshire is another ancient tree believed to be between 800 and 1000 years old, and was said to be the hiding place of Robin Hood.

It was the day before Christmas Eve 1991 when Ray and I nearly came to grief. I'd just returned from a holiday in Florida. There I had found the ideal antidote for Chalky's constant gibbering – a can of bullshit repellent, guaranteed to prevent chronic B.S. It was supposed to cure all B.S. symptoms, including tall stories, exaggerated claims, or just plain B.S. We'd all gathered together at the Rolls Royce conference centre, winding down ready for the

Christmas holiday. The plan was to ambush Chalky at break time, corner him in the gardener's shed, and hit him with a dose. It was our last hope. We studied the directions carefully; knowing there would only be one chance, for everyone's sake, we had to get it right. The plan went perfectly; Ray caught his attention, while I gave a quick squirt to his arm, hitting him between the shoulder and his elbow. He looked concerned, and asked what I was up to, as the liquid ran down his arm. I assured him it was harmless, just clear water without any smell but he didn't believe me, so Chalky, the silly sod, lifted his elbow to his nose to smell it, and in the process, tipped a mug of hot coffee straight into his lap, sending him off like a Jack-in-a-box all around the shed and out into the garden. Fortunately no harm was done, but unfortunately for us the B.S. repellent didn't work. Even a triple flutter blast of three short bursts had no effect. The seemingly 100 per cent guaranteed reliability of the famous liquid had certainly met its match with Chalky.

By eleven, everyone had gone home, eager to do any last minute Christmas shopping, leaving Ray and I to finish off the last of the clearing up. It was unusual, but we decided to sit in Ray's Range Rover to have our break rather than walk up to the shed, a decision that nearly cost us our lives. The grounds have a collection of mature trees, including a magnificent Cedar of Lebanon. There are many other specimens, such as silver firs from Europe, and acacias and Wellingtonias from America.

One of these trees, a copper beech, had stood there for over 200 years. It looked perfectly healthy but looks are deceiving, because now its long life was about to come to an end in a dramatic fashion. It seemed a normal December day, cold and a little breezy with the occasional shower. There was no warning, no crack of timber or gust of wind, just the movement of the trunk heading towards us. 'Quick!' was all I could say to Ray, who didn't see it coming. It was all over in a flash. We sat there for a few moments in stunned silence. Ray's motor was completely crushed but by some miracle, we were still alive. The only injury was a slight cut on my thumb caused by flying glass when the windscreen shattered. I asked Ray if he was OK. 'I'm all right. Are you?' 'No, I've spilt my coffee,' I said, trying to make light of the situation. We sat there for a few moments, trying to figure a way out; Ray was bent double from the impact of the trunk as it crushed the driver's door and seat. I'd managed to open the passenger door, but only just.

We made our way out through the broken windscreen just as the butcher turned up, who was on his way to the house to make a delivery – a minute or so earlier and he would have surely been killed as the main body of the tree crashed down on to the driveway. Some of its branches were driven deep in to the ground. The Range Rover was under tons of timber. Even the tow bar had been buried in the ground. A small crane was used to lift the main trunk, which had to be cut up and moved. Amazingly, the tyres that had looked completely flat came back into shape. The suspension that seemed squashed was back to normal. After lying crushed under that great weight for a week or more, we were able to push it away with ease. We were headline news, second only to President Gorbachev of Russia, who was about to resign. Ray had a letter from Rover who had heard about the incident and were keen to show off the robustness of their motors. We'd had a lucky escape – and it wouldn't be the last.

An ancient oak used to stand in Kedleston Park, close to the visitor car park. This noble and solitary giant must have stood for 500 years or more. Then one spring morning, suddenly and without warning another long life came to an end. The weather was perfect, sunny and warm, with not a breath of wind to rustle the trees, bird song was crisp and clear, and with spring bursting all around in delicate shades of green, it felt good to be alive. Fred and I made our way across the park, heading for the family's vegetable patch. Our route took us past the old oak, one of a few old timers still left on the estate. There's many a time I've stood gazing in admiration of its size and age; it almost seemed like an old friend. This time there was much to do, so we pressed on. Suddenly, the morning peace was shattered by a noise so loud and frightening, it shook Fred and I down to our boots. My first thought was that a plane had crashed behind us. We turned to see rabbits running across the park, fleeing from upturned roots. For no apparent reason the old oak had fallen over, its mighty boughs crushed under its great weight. Even on its side the trunk towered above our heads, its new-born leaves about the size of a thumb nail, beginning to burst for the last time. What had killed this seemingly healthy tree? Oaks can live for 1,000 years or more; this one was barely middle aged, but one look at its upturned root and the cause was obvious. Honey fungus or some other parasitic fungi had been eating away at it for years and it was rotten to the core. It had been another close call; if we had been a minute a so later we would have passed right under where the old oak fell.

You couldn't help but feel a little moved by the occasion. Even Fred seemed a little emotional as we reflected on the changes it had seen and the times it had lived through. Perhaps it had gazed upon the medieval manor house. It would have seen the arrival of Bonnie Prince Charlie's army in 1745 as they came marching along the old turnpike road. It would have witnessed the exodus as the little hamlet of Kedleston was uprooted and moved over the horizon forever. In 1759, another army arrived – an army of surveyors, builders, and labourers. For six years they would toil, building a great house. In the 1940s, during the Second World War, it stood among soldiers stationed close by, and watched as a German bomber dropped its deadly load of cluster bombs on the stabling block and pleasure grounds. Its target was the army camp, Kedleston, which was used by the war department. In 1939- 40, it was a mustering point for the British expeditionary force.

The Oak's Tale

What of centuries past? I have a tale to tell,
A manor house, in a sunlit meadow, speaks that all is well.
From the south battalions march, with ranks that dare not
    dwell,
The Young Pretender's homeward bound, with a story yet to
    tell.
The children have all gone now, with heavy hearts they pass
    me by,
West, towards a new horizon, beyond the darkening sky.
Old Cutler's path is different now, its waters made to swell,
The landscape's changed forever, the one I knew so well.
From the seeds of wealth is born a stately hall,
A place of wonderment and beauty; fond memories to recall.
The Viceroy's now at rest, he made the Curzon's proud,
A gift of Eastern treasures to the hall he has endowed.
The soldier boys and girls are here; heroic spirits fill the air,
Their friendships forged forever, from an age of great
    despair.
From foreign lands a war bird came, its cargo raining Hell,
Again the world is burning; what of the future? Only God
    can tell.

This tribute to the old oak was penned by Fred, just before he
died in 1987.

An unusual-shaped beech tree stands in the garden at Kedleston,
close to the churchyard. A scene from *Women in Love* was filmed
under its boughs. Sometime in its life, the tree had developed a
bend in its main trunk, but unless you stood directly underneath
you wouldn't notice the incredible overhang. Growing normally
for half its height, the main trunk suddenly goes off at a forty-
five degree angle leaving its uppermost branches and a massive

amount of weight overhanging its base by at least thirty meters. It never looked safe; how it had stood so long at such an angle without snapping off is testament to its strength. This time it was Paul's turn for a lucky escape. Whilst mowing under its canopy, he would have surely been killed if not for a shower of rain. He'd forgotten his coat, so he went back to the churchyard to get it. This undoubtedly saved his life, for when he returned not a minute later, he found a massive bough, itself the size of a small tree, had split off and crashed down onto the area he was about to mow, crushing his mower in the process.

In a quiet little Derbyshire valley sits the village of Ireton Wood. So quiet, in fact, you won't even find it on some maps. With a cluster of small farms and houses, gathered around a fine looking hall, times have changed little over the centuries. The hall belongs to the Durose family, and we had looked after the gardens for many years. Mrs Durose had been good to us in those early days when I first set up my own business, always on hand to give help and advice. There was to be a royal visitor; Prince Charles. We were born in the same year, 1948, so I'd watched his life with interest. Our parents were also born in the same year, my mother in 1926, the same as Queen Elizabeth, and my father and Prince Philip in 1921. Both couples were married in 1947. This was also the year of the Royal tour of South Africa, and by coincidence the King and Queen, together with the two princesses, made the long journey south to Cape Town on board Britain's last battleship, HMS *Vanguard*, my father's ship. Apart from having two brothers and a sister, the same as me, two sons, and a dad who served in the Royal Navy, Prince Charles and I had nothing in common. We'd lived our lives light years apart. He was the heir apparent from the house of Windsor; I, a lowly gardener from the house of Elliott, a small player in the game of life. Now, it seemed our paths might cross.

Although only a brief visit, the gardens still had to be made ready and looking their best, including the red clay tennis court. Well-known in the tennis world, Mrs Durose and her daughters had been top players in the past. The court was little used in later years, but was kept well maintained which included a regular dressing of red clay. The dressing of a red clay court can be a messy job, as anyone who has ever worked on one will tell you. The process involves the application of the clay by hand, just like sowing grass seed; sixteen bags of coarse clay, then three bags of dust to bind the surface, about a ton in all, to be applied on a calm day – especially the dust.

Dark clouds had been gathering all afternoon, lightning flashed in the darkening sky, and with a distant roll of thunder in the hills, the signs of a coming storm were ominous. You could see the rain fast approaching, sweeping down the valley, and with the first thunder spots hitting the clay it was time to drop everything and make a dash for it. 'This is going to be a humdinger!' said Paul. An almighty crack of thunder seemed to shake the ground as we ran back towards the shed to sit out the storm.

We both agreed as storms go, it was one of the best. Something was amiss as we made our way back to work. The garden looked different somehow, but we couldn't quite put our finger on it – then we caught sight of the tennis court. Part of the surrounding netting and supporting metal posts had been demolished, flattened by massive pieces of timber, some up to fifteen feet long and a foot across. Some had buried themselves deep into the court's cinder base and with dozens of smaller splinters lying all around, it looked as if a bomb had gone off. I recognised the soft brown spongy bark immediately; it was from a sequoia. Two proud specimens once stood in the gardens. They must have been well over 100 years old but they are only babies compared to their cousins in California, were they grow naturally, high in the Sierra Nevada Mountains. These giants can live for 3,000 years or more and grow to well over 350 feet. I once had the pleasure of standing next to the General Sherman. It stands in King Canyon, California and is one of the largest living things on the planet. At 274 feet high with a circumference of 31 metres, or 102 ft it was truly a remarkable experience.

With the remains of the tree lying all around us, we went in

search of the rest. We were greeted by an amazing sight. It must have been around eighty feet high, but now all that was left was a stump of about eight feet. It was as if someone had packed the middle of the tree with dynamite and blown it apart. When it was struck by lightning, the top fifteen feet or so must have hung in the air for a split second, before plunging down to the ground, where it now stood bolt upright next to its base as if planted by some giant hand. There was no sign of burning or scorching. The summerhouse which stood only a matter of feet away survived intact apart from some of the wooden flooring which was blown from its concrete base. The gods must have been watching over us on that day, as it would have been curtains for anyone in the vicinity of that particular bolt from the heavens.

The Prince's visit went without a hitch and I did manage to get within a few feet of him as he swept in with all his entourage, gave us gardeners a wave, and swept out again, none the wiser about the dramatic events at the bottom of the garden, leaving us to reflect on another close call with the awesome, unpredictable power of nature. Sometimes even the simplest of jobs, without a hint of danger in the air, can catch you unawares.

We had been landscaping the garden of a large house in Milford, Derbyshire. The client owned a successful company and was rightly proud of his reputation in the world of precision engineering, as he explained to Chalky and me one day. 'Our work is so precise,' he boasted, 'we can make anything to within one thousandth of an inch!' Chalky had that puzzled look on his face, and experience told me something was brewing in that wondrous brain of his. Sure enough, after a second or two, it came out.

'Well, that's not good enough,' he said. The client looked puzzled, and for that matter so did I. 'What do you mean? What's not good enough?' 'Thousands of an inch … it's not good enough in our job.' 'Why not?' The client looked bemused. 'Because in our job, it has to be perfect,' said Chalky smugly. The client gave a wry smile and walked off, leaving the man from Kent with a big grin on his face.

It had been a satisfying job, running smoothly from start to finish, apart from the attentions of an irritating little man who from day one went out of his way to give us grief. In the first instance we were at fault by allowing a few twigs and leaves to fall from the garden onto the pavement below. From then on, every time he passed by he looked for something to moan about, expressing his disapproval of the house and garden alterations. Thank God he wasn't around to witness what happened next.

The work was almost finished, with one thing left to do; the felling of a dead cherry tree. You would have thought nothing could go wrong. It was a simple task that took minutes, and a good blaze was soon under way. The main trunk was pushed onto the fire, and being quite substantial, about eighteen inches in diameter, it would take some time to burn. We made our final sweep of the area, blissfully unaware that trouble was brewing. The log had been burning away quite nicely, until the supporting branches underneath collapsed. It suddenly slipped and began to roll towards the steep bank that runs down to the main road. Our hearts stopped, but thankfully it came to a halt just on the edge. We've never moved so fast but then, just like the golf ball teetering on the rim of the hole, before we could get to it, over it went. The burning log headed off down the bank – towards certain disaster.

A million thoughts seemed to flash through my mind, the first one being 'I hope the irritating little pest isn't walking by. If he is, he's a dead man, or at least he'll have a bad headache.' The log disappeared over the six-foot drop, cleared the pavement and rolled on to the road, where it came to rest sitting on top of the double white lines in the middle of the main A6 Derby to Matlock road. We clambered down to find the road deserted, a miracle in itself, being one of the busiest times of year with coach loads of tourists passing through on their way into Derbyshire and the Peak District. We couldn't believe our luck.

With the log still on fire and giving off dense smoke, we kicked it into the gutter. Now we had a dilemma; how do we get a burning log back into the garden? Lifting it would be impossible;

it must have weighed a quarter of a ton at least. The only way back into the garden was through the main gate, and that would mean rolling a burning log a hundred yards down the road, towards a blind bend into oncoming traffic. We had no choice but to give it a try, because you could bet your life it wouldn't be long before the law turned up, with the inevitable consequences. Then we had an extraordinary piece of luck, an unbelievable coincidence, call it what you will, but no sooner had Dave said 'We could do with a JCB to shift this,' as if to order, one came around the bend heading towards Derby. To cap it all, the bucket on the front was just wide enough for us to roll the log in for him to take back into the garden, but this time into a skip.

We thanked the driver, and gave him a few pounds for his help, and if he ever reads this, thank you again. Afterwards, we all had nightmares of what could have happened. That log was a flying battering ram; it would have demolished any vehicle or persons in its way. The thought of a coach coming around that blind bend, swerving to avoid it, and then crashing through the stone wall into the River Derwent on the other side doesn't bear thinking about. It had been a close call, and a lesson to be learnt. As Harry put it all those years ago, 'Don't mess with the trees!' But I never have, they always seem to mess with me. Even when I'm minding my own business, they will find some excuse to have a go. That is why we leave the dangerous stuff to the experts, although it might not always be the safest thing to do.

The experts were brought in to dismantle a Lombardy poplar. Their branches grow almost vertical, giving the tree its distinctive columnar shape. Fast growing, they can attain a height of a hundred feet in as little as thirty years. With decades of experience, and with all the proper qualifications, the tree surgeon came highly recommended but alarm bells began to ring almost immediately. Ray and I gave each other what you might call a concerned look as he made his way towards the tree, saw in hand. It must have been seventy foot plus, and he was about to fell it. Under the right circumstances it would be a straightforward job. This was anything but; it was only yards from a school, and he was about to let it freefall without any guiding cables or ropes to direct it. 'I thought you were going to dismantle it?' The question seemed to annoy him. 'No point. There's no wind, and it's leaning the right way.' To me, it looked as straight as a die. I told him I wasn't happy; 'I think you should at least anchor it down!' This would require him to climb the tree and fix a rope. He begrudgingly agreed but even this, in our opinion, wasn't high enough to give us the required leverage. For extra safety, I decided to use the van as an anchor and with four men on the rope, I gave him the go ahead to drop it. What happened next still makes my blood run cold whenever I think of it. He was almost done and signalled for us to be ready, when a slight breeze got up. The tree began to lean towards the school, jamming his saw. The strain on the rope was enormous. 'Quick! Get me the wedges!' he screamed. One of us had to leave the rope and race over to him. The only thing holding that tree up, apart from us, was about two or three inches of uncut timber. If it snapped, there would be no holding it. His timing couldn't have been worse. Right in the middle of all this panic, the school came out for break. Kids suddenly appeared from nowhere; they were all over the place, only feet from a potential disaster. He was now screaming at the top of his voice for them to get clear while making frantic efforts to drive in the wedges to support the tree. For what seemed an age, we strained on that rope, until at last; and with great relief, we were able to pull it over. The lads praised me for my foresight in securing the tree first, but they were wrong. We shouldn't have been in that ridiculous situation to start with. What an idiot I'd been.

Choosing a life outdoors, working close to nature, it's inevitable that at some time or another you're going to get stung or bitten by some insect or plant. I've been stung once by a bee, had a few ant bites, and stinging nettles are all part and parcel of the gardener's lot. Then there's wasps; they're a different story. These kamikazes of the insect world are a force to be reckoned with.

As anyone who has unwittingly disturbed their home will tell you, they don't take prisoners. I once watched old Tommy Morris as he tried to burn out a nest in a grass bank; they were upon him in an instant, chasing him down the road, stinging him under the chin, while others flew banzai fashion straight into the burning hole and certain death. It floored him, the reaction was so bad, and I thought he was going to have a heart attack. Tommy recovered with no ill effects, but for some people even one sting can be serious, requiring immediate hospital treatment. Ray's arm looked so funny; like a plastic bag full of liquid hanging from the tip of his elbow, about the size of a tennis ball. It seemed most peculiar. It was caused by a solitary wasp sting in midwinter. It almost knocked him out. 'I'm lucky,' I boasted, 'they don't seem to affect me, just a little irritating, if anything.' It was a boast soon put to the test in the most painful manner.

A small willow tree had fallen into the River Derwent. With little rain for weeks the water level was quite low, making the job of removing it relatively simple. The first task was to remove the side branches so a rope could be attached to pull it to the bank. There was no danger at all, or so I thought, as I made my way, saw in hand, balancing along its trunk. Like most trees along a riverbank, this one had a covering of ivy, perfect camouflage for a colony of wasps, minding their own business until my big foot came crashing down on their home. They were not happy.

The whole tree seemed to erupt. In an instant, I was engulfed in the little yellow devils. With arms whirling like windmills, my hands and face already feeling the first assault, I had to get away and quick. Jumping in the river offered an escape but it was only about a foot deep. The only option was back the way I came, across the nest. A journey that was done in minutes on the way out took only seconds on the way back. Ray and Chalky were already in retreat when I reached the riverbank. They watched with great amusement as I ran off down the drive, tearing my clothes off while trying to dislodge the little critters from my shirt and trousers. I looked like a man doing a demented slap

dance. I must have run at least fifty yards before the attack ceased. Now the effects were beginning to take hold. Apart from the pain, my face began to swell, closing my left eye, and with badly swollen lips and ears I felt like I'd been in the ring with Mick Tyson. My hands, arms and body were just as bad. They even managed to find a way up my trouser bottoms, stinging my legs and ankles. It had been a vicious attack, I counted over twenty separate stings on my face, hands and arms, not to mention the damage done by the ones trapped in my shirt and trousers where they had stung away for all they were worth. I gobbled down a handful of painkillers, which didn't seem to have any effect on the pain. It was impossible to rest; my body seemed on fire and I had to keep moving about. I'd been lucky. An attack like that could have been fatal. Whether or not it was down to a course of inoculations I'd just completed ready for a trip abroad I don't know, but I recovered in a few days with no ill effects.

The first priority for anyone thinking of working on the land is to protect themselves against disease, especially tetanus. The risk of contracting the disease from the soil is very high. Having witnessed the devastating effects of this killer on a colleague of mine, it is essential to make sure that all staff have had all the relevant inoculations and are made fully aware of the consequences if they fail to do so. Which in some cases is easier said than done.

One young recruit, Shane, assured me his doctor's appointment was imminent, but in truth we all knew he was frightened to death of the needle. Then a golden opportunity came which would save him time, and give me the satisfaction of knowing he'd be protected against that terrible disease. Whilst working at a nursing home, I met Joanne, a young nurse I knew who was on a visit. I asked her jokingly to give him a jab. 'As it happens,' she said, 'I have one with me. I'll do it right now.' Shane was terrified; so terrified in fact that without saying a word, he went crashing through a thick privet hedge and into next door's garden. There he stayed until the coast was clear. Even the story of my pal Eli who nearly lost his life to the disease didn't persuade him.

Eli was the resident gardener on the Ireton estate. An ex-steelworker from Yorkshire, he was full of 'thee's', 'thou's' and a lot of other stuff I care not to mention. But he was honest and straight talking, and we got on well, and like all Yorkshire men, he seemed to be an expert on cricket and considered himself a bit of a demon bowler; 'If I can't get'em out, I'll knock'em out,' he used to say. Eli had cut his fingers with a lawnmower. He made the classic mistake of lifting the machine to clean it before the blades had stopped spinning – something that couldn't happen with the modern day mowers that have a dead man's handle to protect against such accidents.

After having his fingers stitched up at the hospital, he came back to work. All was fine for a week or so, until he went off on holiday. What was to be a two-week break turned into several months. It was a shock, to say the least, when we saw him again. He was only a shadow of the man he was before. After being stitched up at the hospital, for some reason or another he didn't have a tetanus injection. The disease can take eight to ten days to develop. It struck when he was driving down to Wiltshire. He explained how his whole body went into spasms; 'I was gripping the steering wheel like a madman,' he said, 'my body was rigid and contorted. Every muscle seemed to lock up.' He spent several weeks in intensive care, and many more months recovering from this deadly disease, also known as lockjaw. Eli had found his dream job when he first arrived at Ireton Wood, but like others I've met over the years who have changed careers for what they think will be an idyllic outdoor life with only the experience of tending their own gardens or allotments, the realities of being a full-time gardener soon hit home. The hard work that still has to be done, no matter what the weather may throw at you, soon dampens their enthusiasm. Eli eventually returned to his native Yorkshire and to his people, 'the salt of the earth' as he called them.

From dangerous encounters with trees to nature's smallest

EVERY GARDEN TELLS A STORY

organisms carrying deadly disease, throw in the odd lightning strike, an attack by an angry swarm, and an occasional dose of sunstroke and hyperthermia, there is no doubt the garden can be a dangerous place. One must be prepared for every eventuality, although the words 'be prepared' take on a whole new meaning when it comes to the matter of Pete's bag.

Ten years ago it was an ordinary bag, with two handles and a zip. Just the right size for holding a flask and a sandwich box, with room for a few other items the gardener might need. Gradually, over the years, the bag has grown not in size, but in the amount of articles held within. It's known as the Tardis bag for its capacity to contain almost anything in such a small space. Dr Who would be proud of it. I am sure its contents would be quite sufficient for a trip to the Himalayas, needing only an oxygen tank for the final assault on Everest.

The bag is now causing some concern. Due to its great weight, the bag has become a health and safety issue in itself, with the distinct possibility of injury to anyone attempting to lift it. Even Pete has to admit the bag is at full capacity, as he is at the limit of his own physical strength to pick it up.

Pete's Bag

The contents:

1 coat
1 coat, lightweight
1 waterproof jacket
1 pair waterproof leggings
1 pair individual waterproof leggings
1 pair leather gloves
1 pair leather gloves (small)
1 pair yellow rubber gloves
1 pair part rubber gloves

152

1 pair red rubber gloves
1 pair thick woollen gloves
1 pair thin woollen gloves
1 pair cotton gloves
1 dust mask
1 pair of safety glasses
1 pair of safety glasses (shaded)
1 pair of reading glasses
1 pair of ear defenders
Packet of earplugs
1 pair of spare bootlaces
1 tape measure
Toilet paper
1 pair of boot guards
1 emergency pee bottle
1 diary
1 pen
1 pencil
1 high visibility vest
1 woolly hat
1 balaclava
1 flask
Lunchbox containing sandwiches, and five pieces of fruit
Tablets
First aid kit
Tool kit
Knife
Match stick, with looped piece of wire attached, used for
  removing debris from eyes
Needle for removing thorns
Total weight; unknown, but heavy.

Unfortunately there is a nasty story going around the firm (so far it's only rumour) that Pete may get a bigger bag.

11

They've Gone Bust

The construction industry was a new direction for us, and one in which we were to have mixed blessings. Our dealings with builders had been very little, one or two maintenance jobs for small local firms, Ken Amis being a typical example. We looked after his garden at Quarndon on the outskirts of Derby. Ken had spent all his life in the industry, having built up a small construction company. After years of hard work, he could now enjoy the fruits of his labour; a fine house, cars and holidays. He had always wanted to do a river cruise in Germany to see the massive construction works along the Rhine. Life was good, but it was all about to come crashing down around him.

Through no fault of his own, he lost a substantial amount of money on an industrial development. Ken, being the man he was, sold everything to pay his debts, including his house. He found employment with a local building company and moved into a small bungalow, a far cry from the splendid house he once owned at Montpelier. Ken was to die at an early age, probably caused by the stress of it all. Mrs Amis once told me he was 'too good for his own good' and he trusted people too much. 'It's a lesson to be learned,' she said. 'In business, always be on your guard and rely on no one but yourself!'

In the late 1830s, around about the time the railways first came to Derby, Edward Wood founded one of the city's oldest building firms, Woods Construction. One of their first contracts was to work on the Royal Show. By the 1990s they were one of the city's biggest, building not only luxury housing but also pubs and business complexes. As usual, we were brought in to put right someone else's work. Our first job for Woods involved replanting some open space land on a prestigious housing development at Melbourne in Derbyshire. This led to more orders, and it wasn't long before we were travelling all over the Midlands and beyond.

Working on a building site didn't appeal to me at all, with the constant din of diggers, dumpers and squealing drills, not to mention the colourful language and other expletives being barked out all day long. It was a far cry from the peace and tranquillity of the garden, but Chalky took to site work like a duck to water. He was in his element. Now he could indulge in his passion for trading. Chalky would try to sell anything, and the building site was the ideal place to pick up any discarded materials or junk. After arriving on site, his first priority would be to find the rubbish skip and disappear into it like some giant rodent, rummaging around, emerging jubilantly, holding some useless piece of junk, convinced it was worth something.

Chalky had been away for a while, having just returned from a disastrous relationship somewhere down South. With a child on the way, he had been working all the hours he could, cleaning pipes at a power station. There was a lodger, a friend of Chalky's who didn't work. He was also a friend of Chalky's partner – a very good friend. The outcome was inevitable, and with the help of a size nine bovver boot up his backside, he was evicted from his own house. Homeless, he had no choice but to head north to Derby. There was a sadness in his eyes when he returned; all he had ever wanted was a family of his own, but his depression didn't last and before too long he was back to his usual self. He cheered the place up and made us all laugh again with his crazy antics, or on the odd occasion the boot would be on the other foot and Chalky would be making fun of us.

The gate had been causing problems. For some reason the new

owner of the house insisted on fitting a lock that would have been sufficient for Fort Knox and from the start we couldn't get the locking mechanism to work. Brian had been pulling his hair out and was beginning to lose patience with 'that dammed lock', as he called it. 'It's the most irritating little job I've ever had to do,' he said, taking it apart for the umpteenth time. The Swan Vestas were beginning to pile up around his feet. Like most pipe smokers, Brian seemed to get through more matches than tobacco, lighting up almost every minute.

Chalky came moseying over to observe the situation. 'I know what's wrong,' he chirped, 'all you have to do is...' 'Look, Chalky,' snapped Brian, 'I've put this bloody lock together that many times, I don't need you to tell me how to do it.' 'Well, why isn't it fixed then?' Chalky said sneeringly. Again, he was told to shut it, as Brian and I had another go at fixing that blasted lock. 'You're doing it all wrong,' said Chalky, still trying to put us right. 'For the last time Chalky, shut it!' said Brian, who was now about to throttle him. 'Tea's up!' came the call from the house, just in time. We all sat down to cool off, ready for the next attempt. Chalky was waiting back at the gate, looking rather pleased with himself. 'It's fixed,' he said. Brian gave Chalky that 'don't talk stupid' look, believing there was no way in a million years Chalky could fix that lock, especially after all the effort he'd put in to it. Brian tried the lock; it worked. 'Must be a fluke,' he said. He tried again and again and it kept on working. Brian and I looked at each other; this time we both had that Oliver Hardy look, staring blankly into space. Chalky stood there with a big grin on his face, waiting for our reaction. 'I'm going to beat him up!' said Brian. 'I'm definitely going to beat him up.' 'You can't do that,' I said. 'Why not?' 'Because I'm going to kill him.' Chalky took off across the lawn laughing hysterically, with Brian and I in hot pursuit, bent on revenge, which came in the way of a blast from a hosepipe down his trousers, much to the amusement of the lady of the house. Chalky wouldn't let us forget the lock saga, telling everyone that those two mugs couldn't even fix a simple lock. Some bright spark even christened him Chalky Houdini, the master of the lock.

We travelled all over the Midlands, landscaping around tower blocks in Birmingham, housing estates in Wolverhampton, and retail parks in Coventry. Woods had moved into building pubs for a well-known brewery. All built on the same theme, they were geared up for selling good food in pleasant surroundings. One of these pubs, The Block and Tackle, was up in Bobby Charlton country, Northumberland, in a little coal mining town called Ashington, about fifteen miles north of Newcastle. The job was to take two or three days, and would give us our first experience of working away.

An early start was required for the long journey north. Arrangements had been made to pick up Chalky first. He had to come, just for his entertainment value alone. It was a risk, because his timekeeping had been a little erratic of late. He was now a free man again, so I wasn't surprised when he didn't show. The only thing to do was to try and knock him up, which was easier said than done, as the term 'dead to the world' certainly applies when it comes to trying to wake Chalky from his slumber, as Ray and I discovered one sunny day on the Ireton estate when Chalky disappeared. We thought he'd made his way back down the garden after lunch, but he was nowhere to be found. After spending a considerable amount of time looking for him we were on the verge of calling out the search and rescue teams, thinking he was lying injured somewhere, unable to move or speak. Then we found him, curled up like some giant dormouse in a grass cart, fast asleep. Even wheeling it out of the shed and banging on the sides didn't wake him. 'He must be dead!' said Ray. We literally had to tip him out onto the lawn before he awoke, a look of utter bewilderment on his face.

I knew that if Chalky were still in bed that morning there would be little chance of waking him, but decided to give it a try anyway. I made my way up the stairs of his dingy apartment block. At first I tried a couple of gentle knocks, but there was no reply. I tried again. This time I could hear movement from within – something was stirring. I knocked louder, and shouted 'Chalky, are you in there?' Then to my amazement a squeaky little voice from the shadows replied 'No!' This was quickly followed by 'Shhhh', from whoever else was in there, then silence. I gave up, but before I left, I knocked again, this time to thank Chalky for letting me know he wasn't in, and to say I would see him when I got back.

Ray and I travelled north with Dave. He was a carpenter who worked for Woods and a good friend of ours. His job was to put the last finishing touches to the interior, while Ray and I did some landscape work around the building that involved planting and seeding. We found the whole experience of staying away exciting. We found some suitable digs in a pleasant little seaside town called Whitley Bay, a few miles down the coast from Ashington. There, we enjoyed ourselves on the town each night, all expenses paid by myself. This was to be claimed back from the company later, along with the costs of plants and other materials purchased for the job. All in all, it had been a great few days away.

Chalky still insisted he wasn't in that morning, but you couldn't stay angry at him for long, especially when he had apparently saved the day while I was away. They turned up to do some urgent work on a pub near Sherwood Forest in the heart of Robin Hood country. A small patch of grass had to be cut but there wasn't a drop of petrol left in the mower, and to make matters worse they had forgotten to bring the petrol can. They only had a few pence between them, but a few pence worth of petrol would do the job. With a busy petrol station opposite, but nothing to carry it in, the situation seemed hopeless, then up steps Chalky. His logic was simple; if we can't get the petrol to the mower, then we'll take the mower to the petrol.

Off he marched across the road, pushing a four-wheeled pedestrian mower and parking it next to the pump. He squirted in thirty pence worth of fuel and went inside to pay for it, leaving the mower still parked at the pump, taking up space, much to the annoyance of the next customer waiting to fill up. 'There's a minimum delivery,' the cashier told Chalky. He was flummoxed. 'I'm not delivering it,' he said, 'I'm taking it away.' 'I mean there's a minimum amount you can put in,' she said. 'It's five pounds.' 'You're wrong,' said Chalky, 'because I've just put thirty pence worth in, so there!' By now, cars were queuing and horns beginning to sound. 'Well,' said Chalky, 'do you want the money or not?' The cashier gave up, and off he went, across the forecourt, gesturing defiantly at irate customers. Chalky wasn't bothered. As far as he was concerned, he had as much right as anyone else to park his mower at the pump. Then he had a thought; he'd forgotten to get a receipt. Off he went back to join the queue, to the horror of the cashier, who on seeing him immediately gave him what he wanted, in a desperate attempt to save the station from the pandemonium that that was about to kick off outside. Back at the pump, the mower had gone. It had been sent flying across the forecourt and into the newspaper stand. It was rescued from here, along with Chalky. His mates, who had been watching from across the road, arrived just in time by all accounts.

Woods were doing well, especially in the luxury house-building market. But rumours had been circulating for some time about their involvement in retail and business parks, in which they had invested heavily. There didn't seem too much to worry about; there had been regular payments and I also had a close contact on the inside, a good friend of mine who was a director of the successful house-building side of the company. He had voiced his opinions in the past about which direction the company should be going in and thought they were taking risks on retail and business parks rather than concentrating their efforts on the luxury house-building side of the business – one that they were good at. He didn't seem to be concerned, but promised to keep a close eye on any developments. We were also doing well when we took on another large job for Woods in Burton on Trent.

Chalky was in love again, although she didn't know it. She'd caught his eye on the first day and gave him a smile. That was it, Chalky thought she fancied him, but she didn't. She walked past the site entrance every morning on her way to the bus stop, and every morning Chalky would be there, trying to make eye contact or conversation, but she didn't want to know. This went on for some weeks, with not so much as a glance from the young lady. Rowland the site manager had already warned Chalky about the boyfriend, who was away at Her Majesty's pleasure. 'I won't have to worry about him then, will I?' said Chalky, who still insisted she fancied him. But it wasn't the boyfriend that Chalky should have been worrying about when he decided to ask her for a date.

On a cold and sunny morning in Burton on Trent, Chalky was to make his play for the girl he loved, despite all our efforts to discourage him. In Chalky's case, love was well and truly blind. We all gathered in the cabin for the usual cup of tea before work, and as Rowland put it to 'watch the morning's entertainment'. Chalky's plan was to surprise her, so he took his place on a pile of sewerage pipes just inside the site gate. Bang on time, she came around the top of the street. 'This I've got to see,' said Rowland in expectation, and we all made our way forward for a better view. 'He's a brave man!' said Rowland. 'Bloody hell, Rowland, she's not that bad is she?' someone else said. 'I'm half expecting Wyatt Earp to turn up.' 'More like Chalky twerp!' said some wit behind us. Chalky had to judge it just right. He had to step out onto the pavement just before she arrived at the entrance so as to meet face to face, as if by accident. Chalky's timing was perfect. He stepped out to greet her with a 'Hey up me duck, I'm...' Unfortunately her timing was also perfect. She barely looked up, and with the speed of a gunslinger, she had Chalky by the throat, screaming at the top of her voice, inches from his face 'What's your **** problem? You ugly-looking ****.' Then in one swift movement, her knee was up in his groin and he was being propelled into the security fence. With Chalky on his knees, she was going in for the kill when she spotted Rowland. Then with a big smile on her pretty face, said, 'Nice morning, Rowland!' and walked on as if nothing had happened, leaving poor old Chalky shell-shocked.

It was a Tuesday around about teatime when Paul, the director friend of mine from Woods called. The sombre look on his face told me he didn't have the big fat cheque I'd been expecting. 'How much do we owe you?' he asked. 'Well, give or take a grand or two, around about eighteen to twenty thousand. Why do you ask?' 'They've gone bust. They stormed the premises this afternoon and closed us down, putting a block on everything to do with the company. We were all told to clear our personal possessions and get out.'

Paul looked like he was about to faint. Kath, who had overheard us talking, came in from the kitchen. As usual she was the coolest one amongst us, being more concerned for Paul's welfare than the grim news he'd just brought us. He looked pale and drawn. She sat him down and poured him a whiskey. We'd been friends for a long time and he knew I trusted him. He had wanted to tell us the bad news himself, which was a brave thing to do. 'I didn't realise we owed you that much,' he said. 'Can you take such a loss?' The impact of what he'd just told me hadn't sunk in yet. Before he left that evening, Paul turned to Kath and me and made a promise. 'I'll make this up to you,' he said, 'if it takes me ten years, I'll make it up to you.'

Kath and I spent the rest of that evening deciding on the right course of action. It was a huge amount of money for a small business to lose, and some serious decisions would have to be made and questions answered. Most of our cash flow had been wiped out at a stroke, with little or no chance of ever recovering any of it. On top of that, thousands of pounds were still owed to suppliers for fencing, turf and planting stock. That little trip up North to Whitley Bay that we enjoyed so much with the beer and meals out on expenses were now all on me. What about the wages? Who to pay or not to pay? Should I lay anyone off? A thousand questions were going through our minds.

One thing was clear; banging our head against the wall – or on the door of the Woods head office – would do no good at all. The money had gone, and gone for good. We had to look on the positive side. We still had a good business with a core of loyal customers. I always said I'd never put all my eggs in one basket, unlike some small businesses contracted to Woods who lost everything when the company folded. Others just gave up and disappeared into the night, owing thousands to suppliers. We also owed many thousands of pounds; it was money we didn't have. In some cases it was owed to people we had dealt with for years, some of them small firms like ours. But one thing was clear, there was no way we were going to give up and let twenty years of hard work disappear down the drain. The impact of the Woods crash soon became apparent when I began to ring the suppliers, informing them of our own situation, telling them that all I could give them at the moment was my word, and a promise that my account would be settled as soon as possible. Most were sympathetic; 'Not you as well,' they'd say, or 'Did you know so and so's gone under?' It was the talk of the town, and the list of casualties was endless. We told them all about our predicament. All except one, that is.

As it happened, a meeting with the bank manager was due. This annual event takes place to discuss business, how things are going, and if any borrowing may be required, such as loans or the overdraft facility. The luxury of an overdraft at the moment would be handy. The demise of Woods was a hot topic; everyone you spoke to seemed to be affected or knew someone who was, and it didn't take long for the man at the bank to bring up the subject. 'You've done work for Woods, haven't you, Mr Elliott?' 'A little,' I replied. 'Do they owe you anything?' I'd been up front with everyone up until then, but on this occasion my instinct told me to tell him nothing. My thoughts went back to the days when I first tried to get a mortgage, how that hard-nosed money man insisted on taking my last penny as a deposit. If he knew the truth about my losses, I'd stand no chance in securing a much-needed overdraft.

'The answer's no,' I said. He sat in silence for a while, poring over my accounts. I began to wonder if he knew something; word gets around and he must have other customers at the bank in the same situation. There had already been rumours going around that we'd gone under with Woods. 'Tell me,' he said, 'why do you need an overdraft now? You've had no need in the past.' By now I was convinced he knew my situation but wouldn't disclose it, hoping I would come clean and tell him. I decided to bluff it out and adopt a 'couldn't care less' attitude. 'No, you have it wrong, I don't *need* an overdraft and it really doesn't matter that much to me if you give me one or not, it's just a precaution. I have one or two big jobs coming up where I have to splash out on a lot of materials up front, and an overdraft will be something to fall back on.' After some pondering, he agreed.

Up until the Woods fiasco, we'd been lucky as regards bad debts, with only one notable case (again, it was a builder) who some years before took us for a couple of grand. We swore after Woods that we would never again work for anyone connected to the construction industry, and that has been the case ever since. The only exception being my old friend Paul, who set up his own company and was true to his word when he said he would make it up to me. He did just that.

12

Rolls Royce

'I'll warn you now,' the man on the other end of the phone said, 'it looks like a punk rocker's haircut.' He was right; I couldn't believe the state of the grounds when I pulled into the Rolls Royce training school at Mickleover on the outskirts of Derby. A meeting had been arranged with Colin Clark, a contracts manager from the company's Sinfin A site. Times were changing; Royce's own maintenance staff were gradually being phased out. Retired, never to be replaced. Early experiments with outside contractors had produced mixed results, as I found out at Mickleover.

The site used to be occupied by Nestlé's, a factory producing condensed milk. Understaffing gradually led to neglect and deterioration of the once attractive grounds. The gardener's name was Dave; he had worked for me in the past when I first started up in business. He spoke highly of us to Mr Clark, which seemed to impress. With only one full-time gardener left to cope on his own, a contractor had been brought in to help him out by cutting the grass. The result, as Mr Clark put it, looked like a punk rocker's haircut, and was an embarrassment for a company with such high standards.

We contractors seemed to be eyed with suspicion by other in-house services such as catering, cleaning and security, which could see their own jobs going the same way as the gardeners'. After being recommended by another company, we were determined to make a good impression but it was obvious from the beginning we were just another contractor being put to the test, on trial to see if we came up to the mark. The job was certainly a challenge; the once-manicured lawns were now covered with weeds and moss, and the rose beds that had always been a feature were now overgrown and neglected. The only area receiving any sort of attention was the sports field. After several days of pruning, digging and generally clearing out, the wilderness began to look more like a garden, and Mr Clark was suitably impressed. Impressed enough to give us a contract to look after the site for the rest of the season, and put our name on the Rolls Royce list of preferred contractors.

That first contract in the early 1980s saw the beginnings of a long working relationship with the world-famous aero engine manufacturer, one that was to last for decades. Its name alone stands for quality – the best in the world. Rolls Royce makes the best aero engines in the world, and they are made in Derby. Even if you didn't work there yourself, you knew someone who did. To see that 'RR' logo on the side of an engine when boarding a plane is most reassuring.

'Wait there,' said the guard as I entered gate number five. I did just that. Then he walked over to another car, took a few particulars and went back into his office. Had he forgotten about me? I don't know, but there were people waiting behind me, so I pulled over to the side to clear the entrance. He shot out of that little office like a bat out of hell. 'Oi! You! When I said stop there, I meant stop there.' He wasn't happy, even when I apologised and told him I was only trying to clear the entrance to let people through. 'I'll decide who comes in or goes out,' he snapped. 'Where's your pass?' I showed him the one from Micklover. 'That's no good. You'll have to fill out a new form. Park over there and come into the office.'

My timing had been perfect, having left myself just enough time to get changed, find the nearest wash room, get spruced up ready for an important meeting with Colin Clark and his colleagues. Now I was late. The guard took all the time in the world to fill out the form, in between nipping outside to check on the odd car or two. What had been a comfortable ten minutes to spare had now turned into a rather anxious ten minutes late, so I had to skip getting changed and make straight for their office. I drew some funny looks from the men on the drawing boards as I made my way through that busy office block on A site to a meeting that would open a whole new world for us – the world of industry and cutting-edge technology.

I could see the look of disappointment on Mr Clark's face as I entered the room. He sat with two colleagues, Mr Hamilton and Mr Baldwin, who seemed to be the senior man, impatiently tapping his pen on the desk, looking me up and down. It was Mr Clark who had put our name forward and arranged the meeting, set up to discuss a new contract being put together, and I let him down by turning up late and looking like Worzel Gummidge. Not a good start, as I found out later from Mr Clark. Someone had asked him who I was when I walked through the office that morning. 'He's part of the landscape crew,' said Mr Clark. 'Looks more like the wrecking crew!' came back the comment. 'I must apologise for being late,' I said, 'but some jumped-up little twit on the gate went out of his way to delay me as long as possible.' Mr Clark looked perturbed; 'You haven't upset Fred, have you? Not a good idea to upset Fred...' said Mr Baldwin, shaking his head in disapproval. 'Fred can make life very difficult if you cross him,' confirmed Mr Hamilton.

The company had decided to put all the grounds maintenance works out to tender, not as individual sites but as one big contract. The meeting was to discuss the scope of works, and our ability to cope with the workload in the event of our winning the contract. A contract worth tens of thousands of pounds to the successful candidate. Three or four firms were invited to submit prices; ourselves, two landscapers from Nottingham, and Ron Newton from Newark. Ron already looked after the Moor Lane site and did an excellent job. All the Derby sites were included, the exception being the sports facilities, which along with Hucknell, Mount Sorrell and one or two others remained in the company's domain, a last bastion against the march of the contractor.

We won the contract by a narrow margin. I felt sorry for Ron Newton. He'd given the company good service, but unfortunately he had all his eggs in one basket with the Royce's contract, having given up some work with the Post Office to concentrate all his efforts on the Derby site. He was also at another disadvantage when it came to pricing; having to make the long journey from Newark every day must have reflected in his costs. It didn't seem right to leave the man with nothing so I suggested he kept the sports field banks, to tide him over until he could secure work nearer to home.

Before the Royce's contract, our time had been spent in the relative peace and tranquillity of the English garden. Even in the depths of winter, on the bitterest of days, working in the peaks and dales of Derbyshire with its fine country houses and majestic landscapes was more than adequate compensation for anything nature could throw at you in the way of weather. Working on a large industrial site on the edge of the city was something else, and a shock to the system to say the least.

Working in these canyons and ravines of industry could be a bleak experience. Those early days were spent trying to assess the scale of the operation, clambering over pipes and around test beds, coming across some neglected piece of ground, overgrown with weeds or grass, the wind whistling in between the buildings in places the sun couldn't find – and that was in the summertime. The constant hum of industry seemed to be in your ears all day long. In winter, we watched with envy as workers moved around from site to site on their daily routines, only to return to their snug and warm offices and workshops. On Moor Lane it felt like being in a zoo, with a thousand eyes looking out instead of in, watching our every move from behind glass walls. It soon became clear that working in this industrial environment would take some getting used to. We did have a retreat, a little sanctuary from the worst of the weather, a place where we could rest for a while; Arthur's shed on A site. Morning tea with Arthur became a regular event, as regular as the array of time-keeping machines that adorned the shed walls, once used to record the comings and goings of the workforce.

Royce's people seemed to be a breed apart, especially the older generation, men and women who had spent years with the company. They seemed to have that certain aura about them, methodical, meticulous and precise; proud people who were proud of their company's achievements and its place in history. It is in their nature to expect the best in quality and service. This was the case with Norman Berrisford. We were called upon to do some work on his garden. Although he'd retired, I'd been warned he was a Royce's man; 'he's very particular who works for him, but if you do a good job, you will have a job for life,' I was told.

'What makes you think he a Royce's man, I'm curious to know?' said Ray. 'Well, look at the evidence. The garden is neat and tidy, with everything in order. The house is the same, immaculately decorated inside and out, and look at that old Volvo! He's left the garage doors open to circulate the air, and put chocks under the wheels to free up the handbrake. The car is in mint condition, and it has to be ten years old at least. And if you need further evidence, look at this – I took the lid off one of those old-fashioned metal bins. For someone to go to the trouble of painting the inside of their dustbin ... he must be a Royce's man.' Still not convinced, Ray decided to ask the gentleman and was gobsmacked to find out that Norman had given a lifetime of service to Rolls Royce.

Ray, who thought I'd turned into a psychic, was eventually told the truth.

A meeting had been arranged with Ted Baldwin at another Rolls Royce site. This one was out of town somewhere up in Derbyshire. I thought I knew of all the Rolls Royce sites, but this one had me baffled. I found myself driving through what appeared to be the grounds of a country estate. To my left, glimpses of a river could be seen half hidden amongst the trees; it could only be the Derwent. Wide expanses of lawn surrounded by woodland stretched out to my right, with mature trees lining the approach, I was convinced I was in the wrong place. I'd worked in so many country gardens over the years, experience told me this must be a house of some note, perhaps a gentleman's residence, and a place with some history to it.

I was right about the house. A handsome Georgian building came into view, its red brick walls reflecting the morning sun, shining through the boughs of a magnificent cedar tree. But it didn't belong to a gentleman, it belonged to Rolls Royce. It was their guest house and conference centre and it did have a long history dating back to 1665. It was originally a working farm, becoming a country house in 1758 and being eventually purchased by the company in 1936. It had been used as the project defence headquarters during the Second World War.

Mr Baldwin introduced his colleagues; Mr Hamilton, who I'd already met once before at that embarrassing first meeting on A site, and Mr Stainer, a much younger man, who seemed to be involved in the running of the house. 'We have two full-time gardeners looking after the grounds,' explained Mr Baldwin, 'both are near to retirement, and we have to look to the future. There are two choices; one, we replace each man as he retires, and carry on as normal, or two, we put it out to tender, as we have done with the other sites.' 'But we don't want to do either of them,' said Mr Hamilton. 'Well, I don't want to sound stupid,' I said, now feeling a little baffled by it all, 'but what is the point of this meeting?' It was Mr Stainers turn to speak; 'We want you to do it!' he said, 'We've been pleased with your work so far, and we understand you have considerable experience with large country gardens such as this. Subject to cost of course. The reason for bringing you here is to show you around, let you know how important this house is to the company.'

My brief was to have a have a look around and come up with some figures, but first I had to be introduced to the head gardener

Ron. This was a pleasant surprise; he was another old work mate of mine. I hadn't seen him for years. We used to work together on my old firm back in the 1960s, when I was just a novice starting out. His eyes lit up as soon as he saw me, and I could have put money on what he was going to say. 'Do you remember that cock-up at the doctor's house?' How could we forget it?

Ron had been given instructions to clean up the garden of one of our regular customers – regular to my old boss and I that is, but unfamiliar to Ron. We dropped him off on a misty winter's morning to spend the day alone. Not a pleasing prospect, but the family were well known for their hospitality, so there would be no shortage of tea and biscuits. It was almost dark when we arrived to pick him up, but Ron was nowhere to be found. After searching the garden, Mick said 'He has to be here somewhere; I can smell his pipe.' As soon as we began shouting his name, Ron's head popped up over a hedge. 'What are you doing over there?' asked Mick. 'What you think I'm doing? I'm gardening!' said Ron. Mick was delighted to hear Ron had picked up some extra work in the neighbour's garden. 'You should have allowed more than a day on this,' said Ron, 'I've only just finished.' 'What!' said Mick, as he realised that Ron had spent the whole day cleaning up the wrong garden. We'd been in that much of a hurry that morning, all Mick had done was to point to one of two houses at the end of a cul de sac and said 'It's that one,' pointing to the wrong one.

Ron was a man of few words, an old soldier who rarely smiled and was difficult to get to know. If he liked you he would talk, if not, it was as if you didn't exist. His relationship with his workmate was what you might call odd. Ron's assistant came from Eastern Europe. He didn't speak much either, just the odd word. Not surprising, he'd probably lost the art of conversation years ago, working with Ron. They worked apart, and the only words spoken were in the morning when Ron would give out a few brief orders. They even had their own sheds, where they would spend their breaks and lunchtimes out of each other's way. Whereas

Ron's shed was small, cosy and warm, his mate resided in the main shed and workshop amongst the fertilisers, pesticides and machinery, a cold, draughty place with only a small electric heater for warmth.

If you ever saw a film of Ron's assistant at work, you would swear you were watching a slow motion replay. We've never seen anyone move so slowly. It was almost comical to see him sweeping the drive, looking like some long-legged bird, moving slowly forward as if looking for its prey. With the drive being hundreds of metres long, it took him an age to get from one end to the other.

Apart from mowing, everything was still done by hand, including the leaf clearing, even with modern-day equipment such as sweepers and blowers being available. It was a full-time job in the autumn. Ron and his assistant carried out this mammoth task with nothing more than ordinary garden rakes. It would take them several days to clear vast areas of lawn. Then they would turn around, go back, and start all over again, Ron making sure his assistant worked in the opposite direction.

After a short period of helping out, Ron and his mate retired and we took over the grounds completely. The budget for the gardens had been tight, and there was little money available for extras. One of our first priorities was to replace the antiquated machinery with our own. Next, the lawns had to be brought back up to standard, a major undertaking in itself, requiring months of treatment and scarifying, more treatment and more scarifying... Four large greenhouses with their own heating system were put to good use growing tomatoes and cucumbers for the house, and summer and winter bedding for the garden. Again due to lack of funds, they were in disrepair, and would eventually have to be demolished. The house was managed by Mrs Reeve, a charming woman, and well respected in the company. Together with the rest of the house staff, she ran a tight ship, providing the highest standards of hospitality for guests and visitors alike.

Due to the prestige of the house, careful consideration had to be given to the type of service required, not only in the quality of the workmanship but also in the type of person suitable for the position of head gardener. Ray was the ideal candidate. He already managed several of our sites and had picked up awards not only for his own garden but for a well-known hotel he looked after for us in the city. He was perfect for the job, for as well as being a good gardener he was reliable, conscientious and discreet.

Facility management began to move in a different direction. A bigger fish was heading towards the contracting pool, a monster that would gobble up everything in its path, including us. Just as we had driven out the native species some years before, the emergence of specialised companies with the resources and manpower to run any of the in-house services would gradually see the end of the small contractor. Beginning with cleaning and catering, these multinational companies would gradually move in and take over the lot; security, building maintenance and of course landscaping, with economics and efficiency as the selling point. Why employ your own staff to run it all, with all the headaches involved, when it can all be handled by one company, responsible for all the hiring and firing, administration and sourcing of labour and materials? In theory you could subcontract everything, with only one cheque to pay at the end of it.

I could see the comparison to Kedleston Hall all those years ago. The old school were retiring, people who had been with the company all their lives. Doing business with them had been a pleasure, but now things were about to change and were giving way to a new generation and new working practices. Takeover of the landscape department was swift and within a month we were out. No mention was made of the rights of our employees, on the question of the transfer of labour. Not that it mattered. I had a loyal workforce, and with new contracts to start, other doors were about to open.

We still had the contract at the house. Mrs Reeve had insisted on retaining our services, and for the foreseeable future our position there was safe. Everything carried on as normal for a while, the only notable change being we were no longer contracted to Rolls

Royce but bound technically and legally to the new management company. From now on all business would be conducted through them, all invoices sent to them, to be paid by them.

Now a succession of managers, under managers, representatives began to descend on the gardens. Strangers could often be seen wandering around the grounds, notebook in hand, stopping here and there to examine some plant or blade of grass.

Enter the garden designer, or advisor. Garden design is a specialist subject, a skill not only acquired on the drawing board but also with years of practical experience in the field. Some of the efforts presented were clearly amateurish, obviously thrown together by someone who had been to a few night school classes. One even came up with the idea of making a list for Ray to follow, an insult in itself; when to do this and when to do that. It was clear the list had come from a gardening book, copied from the section called 'Jobs to do in the garden this month'. Ray reared up as only Ray can when I gave him that first list to read. He began with a mumble under his breath, irritated at the audacity of these people, then he came to the 'Jobs to do in the greenhouse' section, he exploded. 'Don't forget to fumigate the greenhouse? Make sure all the pots are cleaned?' Ray was fuming. 'What greenhouse? What pots? We haven't even got a bloody greenhouse; they were demolished years ago!' he screamed, as the list went flying into the bin with the rest of the garbage.

Mrs Reeve retired. She had been very supportive of us over the years and we were sorry to see her go. Now there was a new man at the helm, Geoffrey Temple. With wide experience in the hotel business and a smart and polished manner, he was an excellent choice for the job. Our contract at the house had always been ongoing, the price negotiated and renewed every year. This was about to change.

There was another new face; her name was Heather. Close to the Rolls Royce high command, she was straight-talking and to the point. Under her direction, the house and gardens were about to begin a new phase of investment and development, with the emphasis as always being on quality. A meeting was arranged, and she laid her cards on the table. 'It's only fair to compare costs,' she said. 'For that reason, we are putting the gardening works out to tender.' Four or five companies were invited to submit prices for maintaining the grounds and also put forward their ideas on how the gardens could be improved, together with the cost involved.

Some of the companies invited were national concerns, including the management company who paid our bill. They were desperate to get their hands on such a prestigious contact and have complete control. After submitting their prices, each party was required to attend an interview. Its purpose was for them to put forward and explain their ideas and proposals for the garden improvements. One company didn't even make the interview stage, being told by Heather that their prices were so ridiculously low they couldn't possibly provide the quality of service required at such an important site. Another firm were the opposite, prices ridiculously high.

Although we were up against some big players in the landscape world, I was confident as I waited for my interview, but the situation changed when I entered the conference room for what was going to be a nerve-wracking experience. My legs turned to jelly when I saw the panel of Rolls Royce personnel. Chaired by Heather, they were seated around an enormous oval boardroom table, all waiting to hit me with a thousand questions and queries.

I'd done my homework. A lot of effort had been put into my portfolio of ideas and recommendations. It was well presented with drawings and watercolour impressions of proposed planting schemes. I knew Heather's main concern would be quality rather than cost, and we were awarded the contract on that basis. With it came the order for many of the improvements I'd put forward, including the planting of a new fruit orchard, the development of a kitchen garden, and of course, a new greenhouse for Ray to fumigate and put his washed plant pots in. Thanks to Heather's vision and Ray's efforts, the gardens soon became a place to be admired by staff and visitors alike.

Throughout the grounds there is an abundance of wildlife. Foxes and badgers inhabit the woods while birds of prey circle above and, due to Ray's enthusiasm, countless species of song birds have been encouraged to make their home in the many bird boxes he has in place around the grounds.

There is also a family of resident ducks and they are always on the lookout for food, to the great amusement of the visitors. One little duck, Charley Drake, the brother of Frances, would go to great lengths in his quest for a quick snack. Charley and the rest of the duck family, including sisters Dot and Flo, spent most of their time hanging around the garden shed waiting for the scraps sent down from the kitchens.

There was to be a royal visitor, and with all the top brass of Rolls Royce in attendance, including the top man himself, Sir John Rose, preparations were made for the arrival of Prince Andrew. The ducks occasionally wandered up to the house, and as ducks do, leave the inevitable messy calling card. After a good clean up, orders were sent out to keep the ducks away. Unfortunately someone forgot about Charley, who, on seeing the open door decided to walk in and have a look for something to eat. He wasn't disappointed; there was stacks of food and Charley quacked his approval. In amongst the honoured guests, Charley wouldn't budge until he'd had something to eat and even then he had to be bribed with a trail of cucumber sandwiches laid across the carpet towards the door. With the door shut, the Prince, who found the whole spectacle hilarious, returned to his meal in peace, or so he thought. Charley was having none of it. Having tasted the goodies, he wanted some more and went to look for another way in. No sooner had the guests settled than Charley flew in through an open window, voicing his disapproval at being thrown out. After more pandemonium Charley was eventually ejected for good. What had seemed an embarrassment at the time turned out to be one of the highlights of the Prince's visit. A small ornament of a duck was presented to him as a keepsake.

Ray and I had often spoken about entering the gardens into

the annual landscape awards. We'd been members of the British Association of Landscape Industries for years, but never thought the gardens would meet the required standard. Now after twenty years of hard work, all the recent improvements were beginning to bear fruit and we felt the time was right to give it a go. Imagine our surprise when we found out that the gardens had already been entered into the grounds maintenance category! Not by us, but by the management company.

At first, we were delighted. At last we were going to have our work judged by the industry itself, with the possibility of some sort of award and some sort of recognition for all the years of hard work, especially for Ray, who had for years worked single handedly and managed the gardens on a shoestring. It wasn't to be. Unbelievably, the management company had nominated themselves. They had put themselves forward as the sole contractor, the company responsible for the excellent condition of the grounds and gardens. They would now take credit for all those garden designs and improvements carried out by us and any awards won would go to them and to them alone. For all those years of effort, we wouldn't even have the courtesy of a joint entry. There was nothing we could do about it. There could only be one entrant. We were now technically only subcontractors, and as the main contractor they were legally entitled to enter the gardens under their name.

As we thought, the gardens did pick up an award and believe it or not they even had the gall to invite Ray and I to the awards ceremony, to be held at a posh venue in London and hosted by a well-known celebrity from the world of fashion and design. But only as their guests. They would be the ones to go up to the stage and pick up our laurels. Ray's reaction to the invite was predictable. 'So they are asking us to go down to London, sit around a table and have dinner, and then applaud as they are presented with our award, for doing absolutely nothing apart from filling in a form? Well, they can ****, and I hope they choke on their Martinis.'

It's inevitable after so many years in business; you're going to suffer a few knocks, a few setbacks. At some time or another along the way, you will lose money, you will have equipment stolen, and be let down by people you trust. It's all part of the game, you swallow the pill and you bounce back. But this was the bitterest pill of all to swallow.

13

The Sisters of Mercy and a Horse Called Max

By the time the railways came to town in the 1830s, Derby was a thriving manufacturing centre with enterprise and prosperity driving the wheels of industry. With it came a growing population, as people came flooding in from rural areas looking for work and a better way of life. Many found only poverty, squalor and exploitation working in the Victorian mills and factories. The west of the town was an area of poor housing and social deprivation, with children earning as little as a shilling a week for a fourteen-hour day. A situation made even worse by the influx of hundreds of families fleeing the famine in Ireland. Then in 1849, a small group of nuns arrived; The Sisters of Mercy.

In this bleak environment, the Sisters set up their first convent in Nottingham Road, a damp and dismal place. In amongst the poor and unfortunate, they continued the work of Catherine McAuley, their founding sister. Good fortune came in the form of a generous benefactor, Mrs Beaumont Scarsdale, the daughter of Lord Scarsdale of Kedleston Hall. In a remarkable act of generosity, she donated her own home in Bridge Gate to the Sisters' cause. For over 160 years, the Sisters have continued their work caring for the sick, the poor and the vulnerable, offering comfort and spiritual support for those in need. Their enthusiasm, dedication and devotion to duty are of the highest order, and they are a credit to the town they have served for so many years.

Highfields used to be an oasis of quiet, a few acres of land amongst the urban sprawl, the home of The Sisters of Mercy –

and a horse called Max. He belonged to a well-known local figure, a Polish count, who used to ride around the town. He's gone now and so has the land. So much of old Derby is being swallowed up by the hungry city, but the Sisters are there, and God's work still goes on. The estate was purchased in 1947 and there is almost nothing left of the original eighty-four acres of land. The once proud gardens are now reduced to a few flowerbeds and shrubberies, a far cry from the early days when we first took over. The gardens had greenhouses, fruit orchards and a kitchen garden. You almost felt you were out in the country. For us, who have looked after them for the last fifteen years, there has never been a happier band of people to work for.

The Derby I was born into still had its roots in the Victorian age. The slums and dimly-lit alleyways of the nineteenth century were still evident in the old west end when I was a child, a place where each street seemed to have its own pub and a shop on every corner. Some families still shared water, a lone tap out in the yard, and just like the old days, there seemed to be rag-a-muffin kids everywhere. After the war there was a shortage of housing and many servicemen returned home to live with parents or in-laws. My father was no exception. After leaving the Royal Navy, he came back to live at the home of my grandparents. Although he came from a family of sixteen, he was lucky. They owned a large property, a redundant pub called the Palmerston Arms, and that's where I was born. They also owned the house next door. That's where Dad's sister Annie lived with her husband Billy Legg and their brood of little Leggs. Bill gave his life for his country; he was killed during the battle for Caen in the Second World War. Annie then married Jack Potter, and along came a gang of little Potters. With little Leggs, Elliotts and Potters living next door to each other, and one or two even bigger families a few doors away, it seemed there were a million kids living on Back Parker Street alone.

With two houses there was plenty of room, not only for the family but almost anyone else who required board and lodgings for the night. The building dated back to the mid-nineteenth century, and was straight out of a Dickens novel. The back of the pub used to be the main living area, a kitchen/scullery/bathroom, a place where kids were washed, rabbits cleaned and fish gutted. It was even a place to raise chickens. In one corner of the room there used to be a cage, or sometimes an old tea chest with a single bare light bulb to aid the incubation process. As kids we would watch in fascination as the little chicks hatched out and ran around the kitchen getting under everyone's feet. Out into the yard, the ducks, geese and rabbits provided the kitchen with meat and eggs and with Uncle Joe's fishing talents, there was always a supply of fresh fish.

The room was dominated by a huge table, and there sat Granny Ann the matriarch, watching over her domain. The table always seemed to be well stocked, full of food, always on hand to feed the never-ending steam of aunts, uncles, cousins and anyone else that happened to drop by. The only room out of bounds was Granny's best room, a room for special occasions only, and being a former pub it still had the old bar, complete with Granny's best china and the original ale pumps, a magnet for us kids if we ever got the chance to have a pull at them. The front room windows had the name of Offilers Ales, the old Derby brewery, etched into the frosted glass. Our room was at the very top of the house, a sort of attic room. This meant making our way down dark passages, past old bar rooms, the tap, the snug and the lounge, now dark and dingy bedrooms. Then the scariest part of all, past the old cellar steps – they were the stuff of nightmares for me as a kid. My nightmares were brought to life by stories told to me by my uncles of the ghosts of the old regulars who walked those dark passageways in the small hours. Sometimes I'd wake in the night, sure I could hear music and laughter coming from far below. We'd climb on, up several more flights of stairs before we reached our room, a small and draughty attic room high in the roof of the building. It seemed like the roof of the world to me with one small window and open rafters which made it almost like sleeping outdoors, with all the sounds of the night for company. Lying in bed you could hear the trains of the Great Northern Railway whistling in the distance, building up steam as they made their way out of the station on Frigate. They headed east and into the night, picking up speed and by the time they thundered past the Severn Stars and under King Street, they seemed to be next door.

In some way or another, the Church and religion have always played some part in our work. Whether it was having tea with The Sisters of Mercy or working in some quiet village churchyard, or perhaps listening to Waheed, a wise gentleman of Pakistani origin, as he tried to explain the teachings of the Koran and the Muslim way of life. He lives in the Rose Hill part of the city, just around the corner from were dear old Miss Alison used to live in the 1960s. It was also interesting to listen to some Mormon missionaries as they tried to convert me. The Church of Jesus Christ of Latter-day Saints have a church in the town. It is a modern building with extensive grounds. Their bishop was a friendly man who tried on numerous occasions to convert me, but without success, although on one occasion I did agree to have a listen – purely out of courtesy, so as not to offend him. The Mormons spread their religion by way of missionaries, young followers from Salt Lake City in Utah, sent out in pairs to all corners of the globe to teach would-be followers the story of Joseph Smith, their founder. Two young ladies turned up, all teeth and rather Osmond-like. They began to tell me the Mormon story using a picture book. It was a little embarrassing to say the least, and I know they meant well, but it was as if they were talking to a child, telling me the story of Joseph Smith. He had a vision, and claimed to be in direct contact with the Almighty. They asked what I thought, and seemed a little disappointed when I said 'Not a lot'. But on saying that, the Mormon odyssey is a remarkable story and one everybody should read. Being interested in American history, I wanted to learn more and even made a visit to Salt Lake City during my travels around America some years later. They were founded in 1830 (around the same time as The Sisters of Mercy) in Ohio. Forever fleeing west from religious persecution, the Saints eventually found sanctuary in the Salt Lake Valley, Utah. Remarkably, within hours of arrival, they set about turning a dried-up wilderness into one of the most prosperous states in America.

At the dawn of the new millennium, we were as busy as ever. New contacts with Bass, the giant brewing corporation of Burton on Trent, and one or two new housing associations, gave us full order books. Two new companies came on board, Tarby Construction, which specialised in civil engineering, and JP Contracts. Although part of the construction industry, they were both good friends of mine, and just like my old friend Paul, they could both be trusted. JP Contracts were in the pub trade, specialising in bar fitting and refurbishment. Through them we were on the road again, travelling all over the Midlands and as far afield as London and the South. We didn't mind; they were a good company to work for and they paid well. For some years there had been talk of a smoking ban and with this in mind, pubs and clubs began to prepare by installing outdoor smoking areas. Providing heat and shelter, they were designed to give the smoker as much comfort as possible, while at the same time creating a pleasant outdoor environment with new patios, seating areas and planting schemes. Chalky was outraged at the thought of a smoking ban and, like most smokers, he insisted he smoked less than he actually did – claiming it was around twenty when we all knew it was at least forty. Determined to prove us wrong, Chalky offered a wager; 'Put your money were your mouth is!' he said confidently. Five of us stepped forward; just as confident, we bet five pounds apiece we could catch him out. A crafty plan was hatched. Someone had to spy on him when he made his purchase. As we thought, he bought two packs. The next morning two more, and the same the morning after, so he was on forty a day at least. That was it, we had a reliable witness, enough to convict him and grab our money. At break time we hit him with the evidence.

Chalky's defence was simple. He was right; he did only smoke twenty during the day. The other twenty, he explained, he smoked at night when he was at home. Chalky's natural ability to entertain continued – it seems his well of colourful disasters, cock-ups and catastrophes would never run dry. A business opportunity came his way in the form of a bouncy castle, but not your average bouncy castle. This one was a medieval castle with four huge towers. It must have been one of the earliest examples; it was enormous, and was probably made by some Second World War barrage balloon company as a sideline. It came with its own trailer and generator and needed several robust volunteers to get it up and running. It was soon christened 'Warwick Castle'.

The castle's first booking was for a children's party; it was a disaster. Chalky hadn't done his homework. After struggling down a narrow passageway on Bangor Street, the castle was laid out, ready to be inflated. It was then Chalky realised he'd made a cock-up; the castle was bigger than the garden. With screaming kids and irate parents giving him abuse he had another problem: he hadn't packed it away properly and it wouldn't fit back down the narrow entry. Instead they had to manhandle it over two privet hedges and into the street. With a little practice, he soon had the new enterprise up and running. Chalky was making a few bob gardening in the week, and if he could find a garden big enough, doing the bouncy castle at the weekends.

Then he had a tidal wave. I know it should be 'brainwave', but it's Chalky we're talking about here. 'Pubs!' he said, 'They're the ideal place for a bouncy castle, and with the bank holiday coming up, I'll make a fortune.' Off he went to his nearest pub and booked in for bank holiday Monday, a Black Monday as it turned out, a day that came to be known as the 'Battle of the

Blue Boy'. It would also see the fall of King Chalky and his castle. The pub had a large garden, ideal for a bouncy castle, the weather was good and Chalky and his helpers were there early, roping off the area and putting up signs. At fifty pence a go, he was ready for a profitable day ahead. As expected, around lunchtime a steady stream of families began to pour in, the little ones making a beeline for Chalky's castle. The early part of the day went well, but news of a giant castle soon spread and kids from all over the neighbourhood began to descend on the pub. It wasn't long before a handful of tiny tots turned into a hoard of marauding teenagers, bent on mayhem and destruction. Yobs now stormed the castle, jumping around like maniacs, with little ones being catapulted into the air and onto the grass. Chalky was in a sticky situation and to make matters worse, there was booze, and it was now taking effect, adding fuel to an already volatile situation as he tried desperately to keep things under control. Chalky's helpers soon disappeared, and he was left alone trying to defend himself from a barrage of half-eaten burger buns, hotdogs and pop bottles.

One responsible parent tried to lend a hand by clipping a young hooligan around the ear, but this only made things worse. Off he went into the pub to fetch his boozed-up dad, and a fight broke out. Anarchy reigned. Chalky's takings disappeared and the very fabric of the castle itself came under threat as the mob, using penknives and sticks, began to punch holes into the walls and floor. The castle finally fell when someone sabotaged the generator, leaving poor old King Chalky alone, amongst the ruins of his beloved castle.

Desperate for a break, he decided to take himself and a new lady friend away for a few days. He wanted to impress, so he asked our advice. We found the ideal break – a weekend in Paris. It was a bargain, with return flights at only £30. We couldn't persuade him. 'It's a rip-off,' he said. 'Don't make me laugh, it'll cost you more than that to get there.' In the end, he settled for Skegness. Even that turned out to be a disaster. To Chalky, Skegness was as good as the Far East, so again he asked our

advice on how to get there. 'It's simple Chalky, just follow the A52.' A few days later he was back, nursing a sore head and very annoyed. 'You didn't tell me there's more than one A52!' he said. Now we all know there is only one A52, but Chalky begged to differ. He did as instructed and followed the A52. Unfortunately, it was in the wrong direction, west instead of east, ending up in Stoke on Trent before realising his mistake. The bruise on his head was a present from an irate bingo player. When the bingo caller fell ill, Chalky volunteered his services. A simple job, yes? No. It went well to start with. All the eights, eighty-eight, three and four, thirty-four, two little ducks, twenty-two, then right at the end he called wrong, 'two and six, sixty two', someone shouted 'bingo!' Chalky had to make a run for it, but not before being bashed over the head with a brolly for his trouble.

Over the years, our work had led us to Repton many times, once the ancient capital of South Mercia (Hrewpandum). Famous for its centuries-old school, it lies close to the River Trent and for decades I've worked in many of the fine gardens in and around the village. I've worked in the school on several occasions, at the headmaster's house in the late 1960s and, in recent years, landscaping around the new swimming pool.

This time we were at Easton House, the home of Mr Roger Boissier, a well known and respected businessman, and his wife. Again, we were called in after the gardener fell ill, and what started as a temporary arrangement soon turned into weeks, then months, and eventually into several years. Built in 1907, it was designed by one of Britain's most distinguished architects, Sir Edwin Lutyens, and considered to be one of his masterpieces. This handsome house lies in a quiet corner of the village overlooking open countryside, not far from the historic school. Broad yew hedges guide your approach to the house, with ten golden yew bushes standing like sentinels. Hydrangeas and wisterias adorn the walls, giving life to an already impressive building. The mature gardens offer a variety of pleasing views across ancient pasture, a partly-walled kitchen garden giving the competent gardener all the space he needs to provide a family with a constant supply of fresh fruit and vegetables.

The Boissiers had lived there for over thirty years, raising their family at Easton House. Roger was one of the most interesting people I've ever met. A former High Sheriff of Derbyshire and a CBE, he was a man with boundless energy, inquisitive and curious; he wanted to know about everyone and everything. His charming wife Bridgett once told me that his mind never seemed to switch off. Even a simple task like shopping can take an age due to Roger reading every label, interested to know how it's made, where it's made and what's in it. There was to be a High Sheriff's reception at Easton House and Kath and I were invited, so a new suit was called for. Roger had held the office in 1987–88. This time, the post was to be filled by another family member.

The gardens had to look their best. The guest list included many high-ranking people from the business world, several mayors and other dignitaries, with several large marquees erected to accommodate hundreds of guests. With fine food, champagne and excellent wine, it turned out to be one of the most enjoyable evenings Kath and I had ever had.

In 2004, Roger and Bridgett sold Easton House and moved to their farm in Cumbria. We were all sorry to see them go; looking after their garden had been a pleasure. The fact that Roger had undergone major heart surgery some years before didn't seem to make any difference to his hectic lifestyle; he continued to work and travel the world, until he eventually retired at the age of seventy-seven.

We always said if the money was good, we wouldn't mind travelling, although one enquiry had us really excited – the prospect of working abroad. Arriving home from work one evening, Kath couldn't wait to tell me the news; 'Guess what?' she said, we've had a call from America, Los Angeles to be precise. I was convinced there must be some mistake. I know word gets around, but this is ridiculous, it's got to be someone taking the mickey, but Kath was adamant. 'It's true!' she said, 'I spoke to him this morning. He said we've been highly recommended by a mutual friend. He's ringing back at eight this evening.' There was only one possible explanation; it must be Bill Astle, our dentist. He was a neighbour of ours and was in LA visiting his daughter. We spent the next couple of hours trying to figure out who it could be, excited at the prospect of working for some film star or Hollywood director. Whoever he was, he must be wealthy to be able to hire a team of gardeners from the UK. There were other questions to think about. How much do I charge? Who do I take with me? How do I get the barrow and shovel on the plane?

The call came exactly on time. I decided to ask him what time it was over there, knowing there was an eight-hour time difference between here and LA. Without hesitation he said lunchtime, so I knew he was genuine. 'You've been recommended by a friend of mine,' he said. 'That must be Bill, he's a neighbour of ours,' – but I was wrong. It was a name I didn't recognise, but they obviously knew about me. He went on; 'It's important to have someone who I can trust. As regards the price, I know it's difficult because you haven't even seen the job, but there's no problem with money – all I'm interested in is getting the job done properly.' I couldn't believe it; he was giving me a blank cheque. With the deal done, I went in to tell Kath the good news. She was delighted, and eager to know who it was and when we were due to start. 'Well, he isn't a film star or a director.' 'Who is it then?' 'Someone called Gates.'

'Apart from Gareth Gates the pop singer, there's only one other famous Gates I can think of, and he's one of the richest men in the world. Do you think it might be him?' 'Well, it's definitely a Mr Gates and he said money was no problem.' 'When do we start?' 'He said it was most urgent, and could we have it done by this Wednesday, so I said we certainly could.' 'WHAT!' Kath was stunned. 'I don't want to sound stupid but it's now Monday evening. That means you will have to pack your stuff, be at the airport first thing in the morning, buy tickets, take a ten-hour flight to California, and still have time to do his garden. Unless you have the Starship Enterprise at your disposal, I cannot see how you can do it.' 'I've given him my word now, so it has to be done.' 'Where in LA does he live, exactly?' 'Peach Street.' 'Peach Street?' 'Oh, didn't I tell you dear? It's off Slack Lane in Derby. Mr Gates has a terraced house there. The garden has become neglected and he needs an urgent makeover before the new tenants move in on Thursday.'

She wasn't happy. I was hit by flood of verbals, but after forty years of marriage, one has developed ways and means of defusing any potential flare-ups, a little humour being the remedy. At the first sign of an altercation, I call on my Clark Gable impression from *Gone With The Wind*; 'Frankly my dear, I don't give a damn.' Blunt and to the point. Next, if there is a threat of physical violence, I go into my Clint Eastwood mode; 'Make my day, punk.' This sends the signal that I won't be intimidated. Finally, if all else fails and I find myself running for the door, dodging some incoming missile, my *Terminator* comes into play; 'I'm going to the pub, and I'll be back.'

If only we could slow down time. It seems to go so fast. I can't believe it's nearly five billion years since the world began and here we are in the twenty-first century with so much still to do. The end of the twentieth century found us all well and in good spirits. It took some time to recover from the Woods fiasco, but another door had closed, it was now history, and as always new doors were about to open. The coming years would bring new gardens and discoveries, as well as interesting people to meet, and with the continuing support of many of our old customers we looked towards the next millennium with confidence.

*   *   *

Life seems to be full of strange coincidences. On a trip to London, we called in at Highgate Cemetery, the burial place of the rich and famous and location for many a scene in the Hammer House of Horror films. I couldn't wait any longer. What with the long journey down and the cold weather, the call of nature was most urgent. With Kath keeping guard, I crept into some bushes. Coming out the other side I found myself standing next to an Egyptian-style obelisk. It wasn't as grand as some of the other monuments in this weird and wonderful place, but nevertheless I was curious to know who lay beneath. To put it mildly, I was gobsmacked and couldn't wait to tell Kath.

'Guess who's sleeping here, dear?'

'No idea,' she said. 'A tramp?'

'No it's Mary Ann Cross.'

'Never heard of her.'

'It's George Eliot! George Eliot the writer, the real George Eliot.'

'She can't be the real George Eliot. You're the real George Elliott.'

'I know I'm the real George Elliott, but I still have a problem. You know that book I'm writing? I may have to call myself by another name. Any ideas?'

'Yes, I have a few, unfortunately, but you won't be able to print those either…'